ARKANSAS OZARKS
LEGENDS
&LORE

CYNTHIA MCROY CARROLL

FOREWORD BY KEITH SCALES
GHOST TOUR MANAGER, 1886 CRESCENT HOTEL, EUREKA SPRINGS

THE
History
PRESS

Published by The History Press
Charleston, SC
www.historypress.com

Copyright © 2020 by Cynthia McRoy Carroll
All rights reserved

Front cover image courtesy of Adam Bartlett.

First published 2020

ISBN 9781540242082

Library of Congress Control Number: 2019951861

This book is dedicated to what was but is no more. And to what is yet to come for Beaux Carroll and Wyatt Carroll as they expand their Ozark heritage and move through their own life journeys.

CONTENTS

FOREWORD

Rendered with humor, generosity and an engaging curiosity about all things paranormal, *Arkansas Ozarks Legends & Lore* is a travel guide, a daily diary, a road trip with a supernatural theme, field notes on an investigation, an adventure into the unknown, a collection of accounts gathered in the Ozarks of ghosts and witches and monsters and UFOs—a treasure to share with friends, especially those who might not yet have fallen under the enchantment of those still spell-laden hills.

The itinerary described in these pages was designed by author Cindy Carroll around locations where supernatural events have been reported. Here you will find tips for travelers in search of the paranormal—on and off the beaten track. In the hills and lowlands, the wetlands, forest, riverbanks and lakeshores, in village, town and city, the fascination of the supernatural persists.

This book project really began over a decade ago, with Cindy's first visit to the Crescent Hotel, "the most haunted hotel in America," and her vividly reported experience on a ghost tour. It is fitting that her journey ended back at that mysterious castle in the Ozarks, high on a hill overlooking the village of Eureka Springs, where the paranormal is everyday. The crowning anecdote, among many charming descriptions of eerie places and inexplicable happenings experienced on her return journey, is an account of a night spent in the Crescent Hotel's notorious room 218.

In my capacity as tour manager at the Crescent and Basin Park Hotels in Eureka Springs, it is my privilege to have been invited to write the foreword for this unique and fascinating introduction to the unexplained in the Ozarks. I encourage all who read this book to come and experience the magic for yourselves.

—Keith Scales
Eureka Springs
2019

PREFACE

The pronunciation of the Arkansas state name is mandated in the 2010
Arkansas Code, making it illegal to mispronounce it.

2010 Arkansas Code
Title 1—General Provisions
Chapter 4—State Symbols, Motto, Etc.
Pronunciation of state name.
1-4-105. Pronunciation of state name.

*Whereas, confusion of practice has arisen in the pronunciation of the
name of our state and it is deemed important that the true pronunciation
should be determined for use in oral official proceedings.*

*And, whereas, the matter has been thoroughly investigated by the State
Historical Society and the Eclectic Society of Little Rock, which have
agreed upon the correct pronunciation as derived from history and the early
usage of the American immigrants.*

*Be it therefore resolved by both houses of the General Assembly, that the
only true pronunciation of the name of the state, in the opinion of this body,
is that received by the French from the native Indians and committed to writing
in the French word representing the sound. It should be pronounced in three
(3) syllables, with the final "s" silent, the "a" in each syllable with the
Italian sound, and the accent on the first and last syllables. The pronunciation
with the accent on the second syllable with the sound of "a" in "man" and
the sounding of the terminal "s" is an innovation to be discouraged.*

ACKNOWLEDGEMENTS

Thank you to the following: James Carroll, my husband, a major dude and love of my life; Nathan Carroll, my brainiac son, who encouraged me to keep writing; Sheree McRoy Cowles, my Irish twin, who introduced me to the magic of Eureka Springs; Pam Edgerley, Billye Otten and Jan Willoughby, travel buds capable of hitting the road on a moment's notice; Gerry Dalton, my mother (RIP), who in life perfected the art of flying by the seat of her pants; and my red 2002 Nissan Xterra, which earned the nickname "Elvis" somewhere along a rural Arkansas state highway near Lost Atlantis.

Kudos to Writers of the Woodlands, to Keith Scales of Eureka Springs and Chad Rhoad of The History Press, and to funky people with whom I've crossed paths in life.

INTRODUCTION

Inspiration for *Arkansas Ozarks Legends & Lore* began as a road trip through the Ozarks with my Irish twin during the peak of fall color. As weekend road tripping played out, our good-natured camaraderie fueled by a lifetime of sibling rivalry grew into double dog dares. In short, we ended up spending the night in the most haunted hotel in the country, the 1886 Crescent Hotel in Eureka Springs. On Halloween.

With my six generations of Ozark native ancestors, regional folklore and superstitions mentioned here are passed down seemingly by DNA. What better way to explore offbeat curiosities than with an offbeat writer who descends from pioneers who originally settled the land?

The pages of this book offer a quirky artist/writer perspective developed over the span of many years and fueled by my penchant to seek and find off-the-beaten-path people and places. This collection features years of discovery by way of astounding geology, backwoods folklore and funky people and fine art and architecture—all rolled into an anthology that explores one of the most interesting and understated locations on the planet: Arkansas.

Author's note: Included at the end of this anthology as an afterword is my humorous essay about road tripping to Eureka Springs with my Irish twin sister, an adventure on the tailwind of lifetime sibling rivalry.

Chapter I

THE NATURAL STATE

Have you ever wondered why certain places have energy that calls out to your spirit, beckons your soul? How does a geologic location draw people from the corners of the globe to experience its energy? The Arkansas Ozark Mountains have that energy in abundance, yet the area remains an unsung, well-kept secret.

Most people are familiar with places within the United States that exude a mystical vibe, yet most have never heard of the magic held by northwest Arkansas. Who isn't intrigued by the spirit of Santa Fe, New Mexico, or the red rocks of Sedona, Arizona? And who isn't mystified by the aura of Roswell and its mysterious history? Perhaps the geographically isolated Ozarks have kept anonymity due to an isolated location, yet there are those who have found and latched on to its enchantment. Creative people. Artists, writers and dreamers have discovered Arkansas, knowing it's where they belong. Peace of mind comes easily, spirits soar and inherent paranormal phenomena is a discernable fact.

Through observation and research, some believe the source of creative and paranormal energy for places like Santa Fe or Sedona or northwest Arkansas is a combination of three earth elements: moving water, quartz crystal and iron. Each conducts energy, but when found together, their energy is magnified, as if by alchemy, and mysterious things happen.

In the following chapters, we explore this and more throughout the four regions of western Arkansas: the Ozark Mountains, the River Valley, the Quachita Mountains and the southwest Coastal Plain.

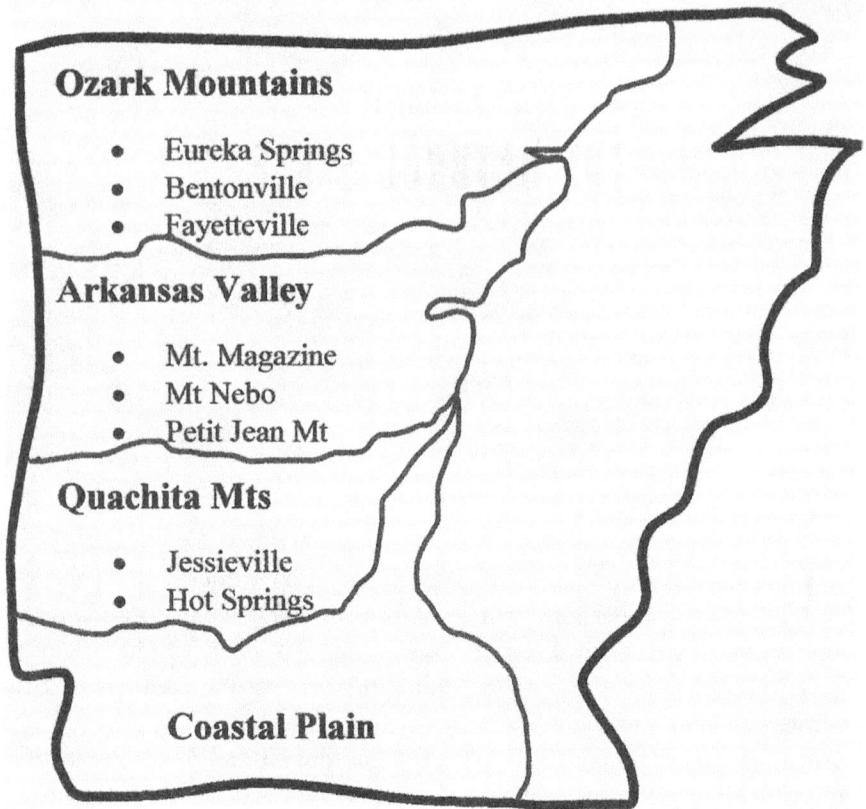

Ozark Mountains

- Eureka Springs
- Bentonville
- Fayetteville

Arkansas Valley

- Mt. Magazine
- Mt Nebo
- Petit Jean Mt

Quachita Mts

- Jessieville
- Hot Springs

Coastal Plain

Arkansas regional map. *Author's sketch.*

HOW THE OZARKS FORMED

Having entertained the notion that a specific combination of earth elements is the mystical source that draws certain people to the Ozarks, the next question is to consider what makes this enchanted land different from other places on the planet. The Ozark Mountains cover nearly forty-seven thousand square miles that span parts of Arkansas, Missouri and Oklahoma. Together with the Arkansas Quachita Mountains, this area between the Appalachians and Rockies is known as the U.S. Interior Highlands. Evolutionary events that make the area unique are multilayered through billions of years, an inland sea, continental drift, uplift and erosion, plus a few more billion years.

Inland Sea

Ancient marine fossils that are compressed in exposed Ozark rocky bluffs tell scientists that the land was once an inland seabed. When continental drift caused the seabed to lift, it formed the mountain ranges we know today as the Ozarks and Quachitas.

Continental Drift

Continental drift, or the slow movement of continents over the Earth's surface, is what formed the Ozarks. South America drifted northward and collided with the southern margin of North America. Pressure caused the land to rise and collapse on itself like an accordion, which created the gently rolling hills and Ozarks Mountains with their rare east–west orientation. The sea drained away, and rocks that were created over millions of years during formation of seabed sedimentation were then exposed to erosion. There are no volcanic rocks in the Ozarks. All are sedimentary, composed of limestone, dolostone, sandstone and shale.

Uplift

The rocks of the Ozark Boston Mountains sit on top of the rocks of the Springfield Plateau, and the rocks of the Springfield Plateau sit on top of the rocks of the Salem Plateau. Put another way, if you drilled through the Boston Mountains, you would find the rock layers of the Springfield Plateau beneath them and, beneath that, the rocks of the Salem Plateau.

Erosion

Over time, water flowing from mountain peaks that were formed by uplift began to carve out small woodland streams. Small streams flowed into larger streams, which converged to become rivers. The River Valley formed this way, dividing the Ozark Boston Mountains from the Quachitas. It is a curious twist that the highest elevations in Arkansas are mesas that rise out of the River Valley, along the northern edge of the Quachitas. Known as the tri-peak area, Mount Magazine, Nebo Mountain and Petit Jean Mountain are flat-topped mesas that offer scenic sunsets and views into the River Valley below, views that are considered among the most beautiful in the state. These mesas are also known hot spots for UFO sightings.

We see the mystique of the Ozarks building on itself with earth elements capable of drawing people to the mountains. We also see the process of uplift exposing sedimentary rock that reveals marine fossils in the U.S. Interior Highlands. When the sea receded from the uplifted landscape, water erosion began to reconfigure the land. The cycles of creation and destruction, by way of uplift and erosion, led to a level of renewal that distinguishes the Ozarks from other mountain ranges, based on the east–west orientation of the Ozark rolling hills.

FOLIAGE

The Ozarks' east–west orientation of its ranges sets the stage for a curious evolution of foliage. The resulting north- and south-facing slopes differ in the foliage they support, based on the amount of sunlight and water they receive. Arkansas might not be what first comes to mind when planning a fall foliage drive, but if you've ever laid eyes on the Ozarks in autumn, then you know they're a major contender for an annual fall drive. Ozark National Forest offers endless mountain vistas of fire color set among shortleaf pines. The sandstone and shale slopes harbor two types of forest: hardwood on the northern slopes and pine and oak on the drier south-facing slopes.

Chapter 2

OZARK MOUNTAINS AND CURIOSITIES

The Ozark Mountains are in the northwest region of the state, extending from the northern boundary at the Missouri state line to the River Valley that divides them from the Quachitas. Eureka Springs, Bella Vista, Bentonville, Fayetteville and Fort Smith are all in the Ozark Mountains.

The Boston Mountains are part of the Ozark Plateau, also known as a subset of the Ozarks, and comprise sandstone and shale about 290 to 323 million years old. Rocks of the region are undisturbed flat-lying sedimentary layers some 250 to 550 million years old. The highest ridges are roughly 2,500 feet high. Scenery includes several high-span bridges and the Bobby Hopper Tunnel, the only highway tunnel in Arkansas, set among oak- and hickory-forested mountains.

ALMA

Located in the Ozark Boston Mountains, Alma is the acclaimed Spinach Capital of the World. A sculpted rendering of Popeye looks out over Alma from the world's largest spinach can (actually the Alma water tower, capable of holding one million gallons of water). Painted by Fort Smith artist William Bland to resemble a can of spinach, it is a celebrated focal point during the annual April Spinach Festival.

ATKINS

The Goldsmith Pickle Company of Chicago set up a pickle processing plant in Atkins in 1946, and Atkins became the Pickle Capital of the World. A popular staple at the annual Pickle Festival is the deep-fried pickle, dreamed up in 1966 as a gimmick to drum up business. Not only does this suggest there is nothing southerners won't fry, but it also gives credence to the notion that the state vegetable is rumored to be ham.

BEAVER

Beaver, Arkansas, is home to the Little Golden Gate Bridge, where Table Rock Lake meets the White River. Built in 1949 by the Pioneer Construction Company, the one-lane, scaled-down version of San Francisco's Golden Gate Bridge is the only suspension bridge in Arkansas open to vehicular traffic. It was listed in the National Register of Historic Places in April 1990. The Little Golden Gate Bridge is located on AR 187, about eleven miles north of Eureka Springs.

BENTONVILLE

With all of Bentonville's recent cultural achievements, it is also noted for native Randy Ober, a seven-time tobacco-spitting champion. He set the record of fifty-three feet, three inches and then got religion and gave it up. As a church deacon, he thought the image was not real good, although he admits to being tempted by that cherry seed–spitting thing.

BERRYVILLE

Cosmic Caverns, discovered in 1845, is one of the top ten show caves in the country. At a constant sixty-two degrees year-round, guided walking tours are popular. The cave is noted for its blind albino salamanders and spectacular Helictite formations that spiral in the section known as Silent

Splendor. The cavern is located on AR 21 North in Berryville, about halfway between Eureka Springs and Branson, Missouri.

BOLES

Giant slabs of rock, known as erratics, were first discovered here by geologist H.D. Miser in 1920. The geological enigmas known as Boles Boulders differ in age and composition from any other local shale and sandstone. The boulders broke off the continental shelf at what is now Crawford County and slid down to Boles, resting in the mud at the base of the continental slope. They're off the right side of U.S. 71 about a mile and a half west/southwest of Y City.

BUFFALO RIVER

The Buffalo River is nestled in the Arkansas Ozarks and originates high in the Boston Mountains. Over its course, the Buffalo drops steadily to its confluence with the White River. The gradient is steep, and the water moves faster along the upper river, leveling and slowing as the river runs its course. Quiet stretches characterize the lower two-thirds of the Buffalo.

It comes as a surprise that the Buffalo, while surrounded by the progress of civilization, has escaped change. Preserving the river as free flowing, it was designated as a National River by Congress in 1972. Floating down the preserved Buffalo delivers a sense of its ancient wildness.

Buffalo River bluffs are the Ozarks' highest, reaching 440 feet above the river. The bluffs are stacked ancient seabeds that have been sculpted by erosion. These multicolored cliffs tower over the river and accent the wild mountain beauty. The park's geology, with its numerous caves, sinkholes, waterfalls, springs and interesting rock formations, defines the Arkansas Ozarks.

In the Ozarks, various wildlife species of the Southwest, Northeast and Southeast mix with ice age remnants, such as armadillos, roadrunners and scorpions that coexist with lichens characteristic of Arctic tundra. The river is currently home to fifty-nine species of clearwater fish.

The forest is home to mammals such as whitetail deer, raccoon, opossum, bobcat, mink, beaver and gray fox squirrels. Elk that were reintroduced in recent years by the Arkansas Game and Fish Commission appear to have established themselves on the upper river. Black bear and mountain lions, once rare, are now being reported more frequently.

The Buffalo River area's rich human history dates back more than ten thousand years. Prehistoric sites can be found throughout the park, ranging from bluff shelters once occupied by Archaic Indians, to cabins built by early settlers, to existing homes of Ozark farmers still living in harmony with the land. Now listed in the National Register of Historic Places, Boxley Valley, the Parker-Hickman Farmstead at Erbie, the CCC-built structures at Buffalo Point and the Rush mining district are protected cultural and artifact sites.

Buffalo National River offers many guided hiking options, with guides available at any ranger station. Short, day-use trails are located at Lost Valley, Pruitt, Tyler Bend and Buffalo Point, among other locations. For the more adventuresome, there are numerous trails leading into the Ponca and Lower Buffalo Wilderness areas.

A river-long trail is under construction, with twenty-six miles completed between Ponca and Pruitt, along the upper river. River hiking often requires fording the river, a difficult task that should not be attempted during high water. Cross-country hiking is best in winter, when undergrowth is sparse and snakes, ticks and chiggers are dormant.

Few experiences can compare to a float trip down the Buffalo. Clean waters, high bluffs, wooded hillsides and myriad seasonal wildflowers conspire to turn city lovers into nature enthusiasts. Inexperienced beginners can negotiate slow-moving river sections. Between Carver and Woolum and below Rush, the river offers a near-wilderness experience. From Steel Creek to Carver and from Woolurn to Maumee, you traverse an outdoor environment with limited facilities. Only in the Buffalo Point and Tyler Bend areas do you find park settings with modern facilities. Choices for length of float trips also abound. You can make half-day floats, ten-day floats, 120-mile expeditions or anything in between.

ERBIE

When Waldo Conard decided to explore a sinkhole on his property in Newton County, Arkansas, little could he have imagined he'd inadvertently discover a repository fissure over 100,000 years old. It was 1903 when Conrad dug into the ground hoping to find zinc ore or lead but instead found bones. The ensuing excavation produced more than sixty-five specimens of mammals, birds and amphibians. Musk oxen and other Arctic tundra animals, extinct mammoth and mastodon were found, as well as lions, horses, camels, antelopes, prairie dogs, giant armadillos and other extinct species.

BOBBY HOPPER TUNNEL

The Bobby Hopper Tunnel is the sole highway tunnel in the state of Arkansas, which also houses seven railroad tunnels. Bobby Hopper was director of the Arkansas Highway Commission during the time of the tunnel's construction.

The tunnel is located on I-49 in Washington County, north of the Crawford County line, with its closest exit at Winslow, Arkansas. The toll-free tunnel opened in 1999 to four lanes of traffic at a cost of $458 million to build. The former route from Alma to Fayetteville was U.S. Route 71, previously classified as one of the most dangerous highways in America and notably one of the most beautiful. The perilous stretch through the Ozark Plateau (or Ozark/Boston Mountains) necessitated constructing the tunnel to reduce travel time and allow a safer trip where weather can create perilous road conditions while driving through the clouds.

To create the portal at 1,640 feet above sea level, twin parallel tunnels were mined through the mountain in a horseshoe contour. Blasting and drilling through native shale and sandstone hollowed out tunnels, which are reinforced with concrete. Its twin bores, one northbound and one southbound, each 1,600 feet long by 38 feet wide and 25 feet in height, offer two lanes of traffic and shoulder space each way in each portal. Southbound traffic will notice a significant descending gradient inside the tunnel, while northbound traffic experiences an ascending gradient.

Every 265 feet in the tunnel's interior, cross-passages allow five emergency entrances. Not only does the tunnel feature concrete paved openings, but it also has traffic signals, lighting, message signs, carbon monoxide monitors, fire protection and closed-circuit television systems

The famous S curve, U.S. 71, Arkansas Ozarks, circa prior to 1952 when postage increased from one to two cents. *Author's vintage postcard.*

that monitor traffic remotely at the Fort Smith highway department district headquarters.

Is it coincidence that the tunnel portal also delivers the northbound traveler into the realm of the paranormal highway?

HURRICANE RIVER CAVERNS

Hurricane River Caverns are unique in that they were formed by an ancient underground aquifer, and currently they wind up in the Buffalo National River. The caverns aren't for the faint of heart. Awe-inspiring cave formations and eroded rock patterns present nature's handicraft inside the cavern along serpentine eroded passageways of an ancient underground aquifer, known as the Hurricane Branch, which winds up in the Buffalo National River.

Aside from the regular self-guided cave tour suitable for families, three additional guided extreme cave tours for the adventurous caver are available if you don't mind signing a liability waiver. And who doesn't? For the audacious explorer who enjoys vertical climbs, sliding, stumbling, contortionist positions, sticky gooey clay, irregular terrain, tight squeezes, short swims and disconcerting ravine crossings, Hurricane River Caverns claims to offer you the time of your life. These extreme cave tours will undoubtedly test your courage and endurance and are not for the claustrophobic.

Hurricane River Caverns is located deep in the Ozarks, off Highway 65 between Harrison and Marshall. It's highly recommended to check www.hurricanerivercaverns.com for cave conditions before planning your trip.

Chapter 3
THE RIVER VALLEY

The Arkansas River Valley is a transitional zone between the structurally complex Quachitas to the south and the structurally simple Ozarks to the north. Broad prairies and wooded plains, flat lowlands and lakes and wide-ranging bottomlands give the Arkansas River Valley landscape its distinct character.

The River Valley is located between the Ozark Mountains to the north and the Quachita Mountains to the south. It runs parallel in an east–west orientation to the Arkansas River for most of its length, which also runs parallel to Interstate 40.

Three flat-topped, steep-sided mesas, known as the tri-peak region, are Petit Jean Mountain, Mount Nebo and Mount Magazine. They rise abruptly from the low valley floor. Mount Magazine, the highest point in Arkansas, rises out of the River Valley to a height of 2,753 feet.

As the South American plate collided with the North American plate during the late Paleozoic period, the Arkansas River Valley, or Arkoma Basin, developed north of the Quachita Mountains. Sediment filled the basin and compacted into sedimentary rock over time. When the land rose above sea level, small streams developed and merged into the Arkansas River, and then erosion shaped the mountain over millions of years.

Arkansas River Valley as seen from Mount Magazine. *Author's collection.*

THE ARKANSAS RIVER

The Arkansas River is a major tributary of the Mississippi River, with its earliest account found in the narratives of the Coronado Expedition of 1540–41. The river was given the name St. Peter's and St. Paul's River. Later, the river acquired the name "Akansa" by early French voyagers. The name was attributed to Dakota and Osage Indians living near its mouth.

At 1,469 miles long, the Arkansas River is the sixth-longest river in the United States, with headwaters running as a mountain torrent through the Rockies' narrow valleys. It then drops 4,600 feet, creating the Numbers and Brown's Canyon near Buena Vista, Colorado, and the Royal Gorge at Canon City, Colorado.

The Arkansas River generally flows east and southeast, with origins in the Rocky Mountains. From there, it takes an eastward course and widens at the Great Plains, where the channel becomes shallow and nearly a mile wide. After entering Kansas, the river traverses more than three hundred miles before making its way into northern Oklahoma and then the Arkansas River Valley.

ARKANSAS RIVER FISH TALE

In October 1983, the largest catfish fossil ever found in North America was discovered along the Quachita River in Camden, once a bay off the Gulf of Mexico. The forty- to forty-five-million-year-old fossil has a skull three feet long. With its weight at 450 pounds and length at ten feet, it would have made one heck of a Friday night fish fry when paired with a couple barrels of fries and coleslaw.

NATURAL STEPS HAUNTING

The small town of Natural Steps has an unsettling history of buildings, structures and people disappearing. It began days after a local couple wed atop the Natural Steps, and then the groom perished from a sudden, mysterious illness. Overwhelmed with grief, the young widow disappeared after the funeral and was never seen again among the living. Many believe she ended her own life by jumping off the Natural Steps, a notion supported by a spectral woman in white seen strolling in town.

CIVIL WAR SOLDIER HAUNTS

During the Civil War, Confederate forces sunk their own gunboat containing vast sums of gold. In their attempt to keep Union troops from seizing the gunboat, three Confederate soldiers died during the explosion. Their graves are located in the town's cemetery, and legend has it they can be seen on moonlit nights marching to the Arkansas River and their sunken treasure.

Chapter 4

THE RIVER VALLEY TRI-PEAK MESAS

Known as the tri-peak mesas, Petit Jean Mountain, Mount Nebo and Mount Magazine each rise from the southern River Valley floor, along the northern border of the Quachita Mountains. How odd it seems to view the valley from these mesas that rise thousands of feet, yet are not actually located in any mountain range. The area is known for its mountainous woodland beauty and panoramic scenic views of the valley, but the stunning sunsets and UFO sightings after sunset are not to be missed either.

PETIT JEAN STATE PARK
(WITH LODGE AND CABINS)

Petit Jean State Park is an Arkansas icon, a state natural and historic treasure at an elevation of about 1,180 feet. Legendary natural beauty and ancient geology set the stage for this lodging constructed from native log and stone in 1933. Petit Jean Mountain is deemed by far the most charming of the three state parks along the boundary of the Arkansas River Valley. The park comprises 2,658 acres of natural woodland on a mountain setting with abundant unspoiled woods and ravines, streams and springs, waterfalls and breathtaking views. The unique geological formations discovered over three hundred years ago by French explorers include well-preserved sheer bluffs, natural falls and natural bridges, as

The Corridor at Bear Cave, Petit Jean Mountain, Arkansas. *Author's vintage linen postcard.*

well as geometrically sculptured Turtle Rocks and Carpet Rocks. Petit Jean's Mather Lodge is in Conway County, Arkansas; the address is 1285 Petit Jean Mountain Road, Morrilton, Arkansas.

Petit Jean Legend

The legend about how the mountain received its name begins in the 1700s with the story of a young French nobleman named Chavet who explored this part of Louisiana Territory and gained a grant approval to claim part of the land. Chavet was engaged to marry a Parisian girl named Adrienne Dumont. She asked that they be married right away so she could accompany him to the territory. Fearing hardship, he denied the request but promised to return and marry her, and then they would travel to the New World together.

Adrienne disguised herself as a cabin boy on Chavet's ship, calling herself Jean. Not even Chavet recognized her. The sailors called her Petit Jean, which is French for Little John. By spring, Chavet's ship had ascended the Mississippi River to the Arkansas River and the foot of the mountain. Indians welcomed the sailors, and they spent the summer on the mountain. When fall approached, they readied the ship for the voyage back to France. They boarded the evening before departure. That night, Petit Jean became ill with fever, convulsions, delirium and then coma. Her identity was discovered, and her grave condition at daybreak delayed the ship's departure. She requested that if she died, she be buried at a mountaintop spot overlooking the river below. At sundown, she died.

MOUNT NEBO STATE PARK (WITH CABINS)

Although Mount Nebo falls short of the 2,000-foot height definition of a mountain, its 1,350 feet offer stunning views of the Arkansas River Valley below. The mountain has been inhabited since before the Civil War, when a resort hotel was built to accommodate steamboat passengers on the Arkansas River. Mount Nebo was designated a state park in 1927. Most of the trails, cabins, bridges and pavilions were erected later by the Civilian Conservation Corps (CCC) as part of the New Deal under President Franklin D. Roosevelt during the early 1930s, a series of programs during 1933–36 designed as relief and recovery from the Great Depression.

MOUNT MAGAZINE STATE PARK (WITH LODGE AND CABINS)

Mount Magazine State Park in Paris, Logan County, is the highest peak in Arkansas, rising out of the Arkansas River Valley. The mountain is thirty-fourth in elevation in the United States. At 2,753 feet, some consider it the only actual mountain in the state. Mount Magazine is the most dramatic location for rock climbing, and it's one of only two parks in the Arkansas state park system to offer hang-gliding launch areas. Located due north of Blue Mountain Lake and approximately forty-five miles east of the

Oklahoma border, Mount Magazine lies within the Arkansas River Valley at the southern section of the Ozark National Forest.

The tri-peak mesas are among the best the Natural State offers for panoramic vistas and natural beauty. Each mesa is a state park that offers camping, recreation and educational programs; in addition, Petit Jean and Mount Magazine have Adirondack-style lodges and cabins that surpass upscale hotels in quality and amenities. To up the ante, wildlife is abundant in the parks, along with paranormal phenomena, frequent UFO sightings and haunted locations that are revealed in detail on the pages that follow. Stories range from the Petit Jean legend to Mount Magazine's haunted Pioneer Cemetery to Native American folklore, cave paintings and artifacts found on location.

Chapter 5

QUACHITA MOUNTAINS

The Quachitas are in the central region of the state, south of the River Valley and bordered by Oklahoma to the west. The southern lowlands, known as the West Gulf Coastal Plain, are to the south, and to the east is the Mississippi Alluvial Plain. Cavanal Hill, Rich Mountain, Wilton Mountain,

A crystal cluster (weighing 1,500 pounds) mined from the Quachita Mountains, on display at Crystal Bridges Museum of American Art. *Author's collection.*

Lost Mountain, Big Mountain, Poteau Mountain, Black Fort Mountain and Buckeye Mountain compose the Quachitas. Jessieville, Mount Ida, Hot Springs and National Quachita Forest are in the Quachitas. Large populations of white-tailed deer and coyote live among hundreds of elusive black bears.

Anyone who doesn't mind crawling around in iron-infused dirt (and who doesn't) will want to experience the fun of digging for quartz crystals. Local mines are noted for producing some of the best quality crystals found on the planet. Jessieville is known for the Ron Coleman Crystal Mine and the 1897 legendary UFO encounter of the third kind.

When tectonic plates collided about 300 million years ago, the Quachita Mountains formed. Silica-rich water moved through fractures of sandstone under high heat and pressure. As hot water pushed upward through rocks and then cooled, crystals were formed over millions of years, and it took millions more for erosion to expose the crystals.

DE QUEEN'S BIG HEAD SCULPTURE

Big Head by Harold Mabry, circa 1959. *Author's sketch.*

De Queen, in Sevier County, is located in the southwest section of the state of Arkansas within the Quachita National Forest and is home to a giant sculpture that resembles an Easter Island head. De Queen is on U.S. 70 East near the state's western border with Oklahoma. The sculpture is located on Highway 71, six miles north of the intersection of Highway 70 and Highway 71, two miles south of De Queen. It sits about one hundred feet off the road in the landscape. Big Head sculpture is accessible by taking the walking path that begins at East Side Flea Market.

The roadside art known as Big Head sculpture, created circa 1959, stands seventeen feet tall and is made of steel-reinforced concrete. It's the creation of Harold Mabry of De Queen, a sign painter by trade with some formal art training at a local college. He illustrated calendars and did promotional watercolors for a local bank. Mabry denies that his sculpture carries the obvious likeness of the Easter Island heads and denies there was any Native American tribal influence. He just wanted to convey a feeling of massiveness by using planes and angles, so the story goes, and he refers to the piece as Big Head or Male Head.

Its creation mandated four phases. First, native red clay was excavated on site to create the mold. You might say all the iron in that red clay gave the head magnetism. The facial surface was formed into smooth and detailed planes and angles and then placed face-down. The back and sides were buttressed with lumber. Next, a truck chassis and other steel were used as reinforcement, and then a local contractor was hired to fill the entire mishmash with concrete. After about two months to solidify, a bulldozer pulled the head upright onto its base, and then Mabry painted a faux stone finish onto the surface.

Mabry's sculpture is listed in the Arkansas Historic Preservation Program, a division of the Department of Arkansas Heritage. Yet Harold Mabry is noted as saying, "I ain't no damn genius." He is considered an eccentric by the De Queen townspeople, but nobody can conjure a specific incident to back it up. It goes without saying that to be labeled as Arkansas eccentric raises the bar for eccentric people globally. And that's a good thing.

As if to up the ante on eccentricity, the female head that Mabry had planned was never sculpted. Mabry described his concept and resulting miniature prototype as resembling the classic gray space alien of modern folklore. In 1959, Mabry's vernacular was well ahead of his time, because back in the day, the alien concept was that of little green men from Mars. Was Harold Mabry an alien being himself? 1959, y'all!

HOT SPRINGS DISAPPEARING ACT

Some say the Malco Theatre at 817 Central Avenue is haunted. Here's why: during a magic act in 1888, magician Jerome Schmitar chose Clara Sutherland from the audience to assist him. He covered her with a red cloth, and when he whisked it away, she had vanished. When Jerome attempted to bring her back to the physical realm, Clara did not materialize. She was never seen again.

HOT SPRINGS HELL'S HALF ACRE

A patch of barren no-man's land in Hot Springs presents a puzzle. Although it's surrounded by trees and other vegetation, nothing grows on this particular spot. Why? Could it be the crater of an extinct volcano or the top of an ancient rockslide? Or is it actually the Devil's playground, where even hunting dogs dare not tread?

HOT SPRINGS WORLD'S SHORTEST STREET IN EVERYDAY USE

The ninety-eight-foot-long street is listed by *Ripley's Believe It or Not!* as the world's shortest street in everyday use, a distinction the city uses by making Bridge Street the route of its annual World's Shortest St. Patrick's Day Parade.

HOPE, ARKANSAS, WATERMELON CAPITAL OF THE WORLD

The boyhood home of former President Bill Clinton is also known to produce the world's largest watermelons. Hope's record-breaking watermelons have been listed in the *Guinness Book of World Records* twice, in 1985 for a 260.0-pound melon and in 2005 for a 268.8-pound melon. Not to be missed at the annual watermelon festival are the eating and seed-spitting contests and the melon-tossing competition.

JESSIEVILLE

Jessieville, Arkansas, is best known for the quality and clarity of quartz crystals found in the region. People come from around the globe to dig for crystals at Jessieville and Mount Ida mines. Jessieville, and Mount Ida in particular, is noted as one of only two places on the globe that produce crystals of this high quality; the other is in Brazil. Vague legends of caves considered spiritual places to Native Americans exist, but their locations have been lost to time.

At 723 feet above sea level, the rise in altitude is palpable when driving north on state Highway 7 out of Hot Springs. Jessieville is in Garland County in the Quachita Mountains, south of the thirty-sixth parallel, next to Hot Springs Village and north of Hot Springs.

JESSIEVILLE UFO LEGEND

UFO encounters in the Quachitas are documented as far back as the 1897 report of Constable John Sumpter Jr. and Deputy Sheriff John McLembre coming upon an airship in Garland County while they were looking for cattle rustlers.

It was May 6, 1897, in the Quachita Mountains in the area of Jessieville. The constable and his deputy sheriff were riding horseback, headed northwest over Blue Quachita Mountain at Jessieville, when they saw a bright light in the sky. The light disappeared behind a hilltop, then reappeared and descended closer to the earth. When it again disappeared, the horses halted and refused to continue.

When the two officers saw people moving around in the darkness, they drew weapons and approached the shadowy figures. The officers demanded these strangers identify themselves. A mysterious man approached them and explained that he and two companions were traveling the country in an airship. He tried to coax them aboard the sixty-foot cigar-shaped object, but the constable and deputy refused. When they returned later that night, there was no trace of the ship or its peculiar occupants.

Local people can't seem to agree whether Jessieville has ghosts or not. Some say there is no way Jessieville has ghosts, while others claim to have had encounters with spirits. There is no infamous haunting that I could find documented, but logic dictates that with all the quartz crystal embedded in iron-rich soil, there must be something paranormal going on in this part of Arkansas. Perhaps the locals are hybrid aliens/humans and don't want that secret to get out.

RICH MOUNTAIN'S LOVERS' LEAP

Each year at the peak of fall color, an older couple travels to Rich Mountain to retreat at the Queen Wilhelmina lodge and enjoy the scenery of the mountains and River Valley. He is a natural-born storyteller who easily pulls other visitors into the energy of his spontaneous and magnetic delivery of an anecdote. Likewise, it's safe to assume that his wife is a good sport.

His comic storytelling style is very old school, like a segment on *The Tonight Show Starring Johnny Carson*. Perfectly groomed from head to toe, with shirt and slacks showing starched creases of a professional caliber, his vintage men's aftershave brings back vague childhood memories that transport one back decades simply by the ephemeral smell of it.

High atop Rich Mountain at the Queen Wilhelmina lodge, he stands straight, with shoulders back, and then takes a deep breath and says, "I like to come here every fall, just me and my wife. I took her over to Lovers' Leap about five times last year. But she still wouldn't. So then I drove her to Lovers' Lane after that, over on the other side of the mountain at the overlook at sunset. I parked the car and asked her if she'd like to get in the back seat. She looked puzzled and maybe a little angry, then emphatically said that she would not like to get in the back seat. She'd rather stay in front with me."

The small audience that had gathered around to listen to this man's stories wondered if they'd met a time traveler or ghost from another era with a penchant for off-color jokes.

RICH MOUNTAIN'S GIANT, STINKING, GLOWING EARTHWORM

On June 11, 1973, Dr. Bruce Means, PhD, was out digging for salamanders on Rich Mountain in Polk County, Arkansas (location of Queen Wilhelmina State Park), when he discovered the second-largest earthworm ever found in the United States, at two feet in length.

In addition to being notable for its exceptionally large size, this earthworm secretes distasteful fluid that glows in the dark. Research does not reveal how the secreted glowing fluid is known as bad tasting, and perhaps that is best left unsaid. However, one cannot help but wonder if there is a connection to Rich Mountain's allegedly haunted Pioneer Cemetery, established during the Civil War.

The species, known as diplocardia meansi, is a nocturnal creature known to exist only in Rich Mountain's dry soils and rocky slopes. Rainy nights during April and May will draw out these giant earthworms in large numbers, where they have been observed crossing the mountain highway at night, likely trolling for mates.

Why would anyone be out searching for salamanders on Rich Mountain? Dr. Bruce Means, bearing the psychological weight of having a giant, glowing, bad-tasting worm named after him, is the president and executive director of the Coastal Plains Institute and Land Conservancy, dedicated to conserving the rich biodiversity of the vast Coastal Plain of the United States. His research includes the evolution and natural history of amphibians and reptiles. The giant worm species was named after Means in 1977.

RICH MOUNTAIN'S HAUNTED PIONEER CEMETERY

Rich Mountain's haunted Pioneer Cemetery dates back to the Civil War, when a few pioneer families settled along the rocky crest of Rich Mountain. Times were hard for these refugees hoping to escape the horrors of war in the lowlands. A desperate mother, sick with severe fever, sent her teenage daughter to get water from a nearby spring during a relentless snowstorm, but the girl never returned to their cabin. Hungry wolves cornered her in a tree, and she froze to death. The young girl is buried in Rich Mountain Pioneer Cemetery on the slope of Rich Mountain, where her spirit roams.

For taphophile travelers, note that the sparse little cemetery has groups of family plots that include a lot of babies. Tombstones are weatherworn and simple in style; some merely use stones as markers. Strange lights have been seen in the trees on this isolated mountain slope where there is no electricity, and EVP recorders have picked up a child's voice calling "mommy" and have recorded a female voice singing a lullaby. Orbs sometimes appear in photographs of the cemetery.

This type of family exchange comes from a time when the rural Arkansas population was sparse and life was full of hardship. Perhaps the spirit of Rich Mountain Pioneer Cemetery inspired the 1938 play by Thornton Wilder titled *Our Town*, the fictional story of a small American town as told through the interred of the town's graveyard. The play is set on a mostly bare stage, eerily like the simple setting of the Pioneer Cemetery on Rich Mountain.

Haunted or not, it is best to be moving down the mountain by dusk, when the veil between our worlds thins and allows the passage of spirits.

To get to the cemetery, take Talimena Scenic Drive west of Queen Wilhelmina State Park, then look for an interpretive sign and short trail leading to historic Rich Mountain Pioneer Cemetery.

UFO Sighting on Rich Mountain

Staying outdoors well after sunset atop Rich Mountain may just alter your perception of UFOs. Why, you say? Well, when the sky is velvet-black and the stars are visible, strange things happen in the sky. On the south side of the mesa that houses the Queen Wilhelmina lodge where the sky is darkest over the River Valley, the stars appear to move around in quick, erratic patterns. They appear to move up and down, side to side and sometimes on the diagonal, but always with quick gestural movement, as if jumping from one spot to another. They move one at a time or in multiples in various locations. The night sky over Rich Mountain looks like an otherworldly pinball convention in the sky. Stellar!

Chapter 6

THE COASTAL PLAIN

The Arkansas Coastal Plain was covered by Gulf of Mexico water up until about 50 million years ago when the landmass rose with tectonic uplift, revealing terrain that is mostly flat bedrock covered with sediment composed of sand and gravel. The visible boundary where the Coastal Plain meets the Quachita Mountains is known as a fall line. Surface deposits, sand and clay with lignite and quartzite limestone of ocean origin date back 135 million years.

ARKADELPHIA

Given that Arkadelphia is home of the Quachita Baptist University, it might be hard to believe that in 1932, *Ripley's Believe It or Not!* singled out the city as having more gas stations than churches.

CRATER OF DIAMONDS STATE PARK

The Crater of Diamonds State Park near Murfreesboro in Pike County is located near the fall line where the Gulf Coastal Plain meets the Quachita Mountains. Crater of Diamonds, established in 1972, is the only such crater in the United States. The largest diamond ever found at this site measures 16.37 carats. Diamonds are valuable because they are rare. A narrow window of conditions is required to form them and send them to Earth's surface. They are the solid form of carbon in a crystal structure and form where carbon, temperature and pressure align about one hundred miles below the earth's crust. They spew to the surface through a volcanic pipe during a volcanic eruption.

GURDON LIGHT

Near the town of Gurdon, Arkansas, a mysterious light can be seen floating among the trees. The Gurdon Light glows white-blue, green or orange and bobs through the trees near the railroad tracks in a remote wooded area.

The Gurdon Light is located about seventy-five miles south of Little Rock, off Interstate 30 and just east of Interstate 67 in southern Arkansas. A trial run to find the location is strongly recommended. Don't attempt this in the dark; the exact location of the moving lights can vary, and getting there is tricky because the railroad tracks are still used by trains. After parking your car at the intersection near the railroad tracks, you'll walk down the tracks about two miles and cross four creek bridges. There may be crocodiles and snakes, for starters. Not for the faint of heart!

Some scientists suggest the lights are caused by the piezoelectric effect, which is electricity generated by pressurized quartz crystals located in the ground. Crystals under stress can glow. Unlike other mysterious lights, the Gurdon Light is reported to be present both day and night. *Unsolved Mysteries* profiled the phenomenon on episode #202, which aired on December 16, 1994.

Local legend has it that the light is the lantern of a railroad worker who fell on the tracks and was beheaded. You might say he lost his head, but why would a beheaded worker even need a lantern? I mean, really. Consider the geologic anomaly as the cause of the mystery lights. Once again, the mix of running water, quartz crystal and iron railroad tracks creates paranormal alchemy.

GURDON HOO-HOO

While checking out the Gurdon Mystery Lights, stop in at 207 Main Street to check out the Hoo-Hoo Museum. Its legacy began as a parody of fraternal organizations. The group features the number nine. Famous people with ties to the Hoo-Hoos include former president Theodore Roosevelt (#999) and Elizabeth Taylor, who was named Miss Hoo-Hoo in 1948.

ELEPHANT SANCTUARY

Your eyes are not playing tricks; there really is an elephant sanctuary in the Coastal Plain of Arkansas. Riddle's Elephant and Wildlife Sanctuary was established by Scott and Heidi Riddle in 1990 on 330 acres in the Ozark Mountain foothills. It's an internationally recognized nonprofit organization that is home to elephants needing sanctuary for any reason regardless of species, gender or disposition. It seems that even those blustery elephants that do not work or play well with others are welcome here.

The sanctuary is funded entirely by private donations, so contributions (including in-kind donations such as building materials and equipment) are always welcome. Call ahead for information about visiting the refuge, located at Arkansas 25 off U.S. 65 North in Greenbrier, Arkansas.

MAGNET COVE

What is now known as Arkansas was a hotbed of volcanic activity 100 million years ago that formed the Crater of Diamonds and the lesser-known Magnet Cove, a volcanic intrusion about five miles in diameter. When hot magma didn't reach the surface, the hot vapors condensed into veins of magnetic ore.

Located twelve miles southeast of Hot Springs, what makes Magnet Cove unique in the world is that it contains more minerals in its five-mile radius than any other spot on earth. Of the seventy-five known minerals, some are found only in two other locations on the planet: the Ural Mountains in Russia and the Tyrolean Alps in western Austria and northern Italy.

NATIVE AMERICAN FOLKLORE OF THE COASTAL PLAIN

An ancient myth of Native American tradition, long before early settlers discovered the springs and their healing powers, tells of an ancient time when the Caddo tribe populated the Quachita Mountains and enjoyed the fruit of the mountain in great abundance.

When a fierce dragon invaded and devastated the land, it brought sickness and famine to the Caddo tribe and greatly disturbed the Great Spirit who resided in the forest. The Indian nations pleaded with the Great Spirit to subdue the dragon. The Spirit summoned heavenly forces to bury the dragon deep under the mountain and restore paradise to the Caddo tribe. The once abundant forest regained its bounty, and birdsong again traveled along the peaceful hills on the wind. The Great Spirit restored his beautiful resting spot and caused hot healing waters to gush from the earth. To this day, the dragon continues to shake the earth.

ROYAL, ARKANSAS

The grave of Texas-born Daniel Richmond Edwards in Cunningham Cemetery (Garland County, Royal, Arkansas) is noted by *Ripley's Believe It or Not!* Edward served in both World War I and World War II and is noted by *Ripley's* as one of the most decorated American soldiers of all time. Among his accolades are the Silver Star, the Distinguished Service Cross and the Congressional Medal of Honor. He was wounded fifty-five times in combat.

THE TEXARKANA FOUKE MONSTER

In early May 1971, Bobby Ford turned up in a Texarkana emergency room for treatment of injuries. About one week after moving to a new home, Ford began hearing strange noises at night that sounded like something was circling the house. One Saturday evening, something reached through a window and pawed his wife. The intruder fled but returned around midnight. When Ford went outside to investigate, the creature hurled him to the ground. Ford described it as a hairy, seven-foot-tall creature with a foul odor. He said it ran with stooped posture while swinging its arms like an ape.

Chapter 7

THE THIRTY-SEVENTH PARALLEL, AKA THE PARANORMAL HIGHWAY

The theory of the thirty-seventh parallel north as a paranormal highway is the brainchild of Chuck Zukowski, a Colorado researcher who has been documenting paranormal events for more than twenty-five years. He's been dubbed the Colorado UFO nut and wears the label proudly. His interests are UFO sightings, alien abductions, cattle mutilations and other strange phenomena across the United States. Whether he's researching or hands-on investigating, Zukowski looks for patterns of activity that he first noticed in Colorado and then later in other locations. Zukowski and his sister, Debbie Ziegelmeyer, a Missouri investigator, teamed up and pieced together reports of UFO sightings and animal mutilations spanning the thirty-seventh degree latitude north.

THE THIRTY-SEVENTH PARALLEL DEFINED

The term "paranormal highway" defines the geologic band that runs along the thirty-seventh parallel north. The broader definition is the space between the thirty-sixth and thirty-eighth parallels, which spans about 150 miles north to south and circles the globe.

At the thirty-seventh parallel band, the tangible intrigue of the Natural State transcends its state motto when entering the paranormal highway. In Arkansas, it begins at Fayetteville and encompasses the state to the northern border. In North America, the band stretches across the heartland of the USA, through Virginia, Kentucky, Arkansas, Missouri, Kansas, Oklahoma, Colorado, New Mexico, Utah and Arizona. It continues west through Nevada, ending at San Francisco, California.

THIRTY-SEVENTH PARALLEL ANOMALIES

Anomalies along the paranormal highway feature a growing list of eyewitness UFO phenomena, seismic events, natural formations like caves, man-made structures such as military bases, animal mutilations and sites sacred to Native Americans.

UFO sightings have been documented by police in some cities, and crashes along the parallel include those in 1941 in Cape Girardeau, Missouri; 1947 in Roswell, New Mexico; and 1948 in Aztec, New Mexico. Seismic events along the parallel involve significant earthquakes. Consider the 1811–12 New Madrid, Missouri quakes; the 1906 San Francisco earthquake; and the 2011 Fukushima, Japan disaster. The New Madrid quakes, the worst in the recorded history of the globe, delivered astounding events. The laws of nature seemed upside-down, and those affected by the quakes feared the world was coming to an end when the Mississippi River reversed its flow. Pressurized quartz crystal produced earthquake lights, a natural phenomenon known as seismoluminescence. A mysterious earth hum is heard in Taos, New Mexico. There is no apparent cause for the hum, which randomly comes and goes and is heard by some but not all people.

Natural formations along the parallel include massive cave systems, such as Kentucky's Mammoth Cave, Oklahoma's Alabaster Cavern and Arizona's Grand Canyon. The Missouri and Arkansas Ozarks have countless cave systems. Some theorize that sophisticated underground tunnel systems connect the caves. Some believe alien bases connect with our military bases via the tunnel system, claiming the technology to create such an extensive tunnel system exists in our time. Man-made structures near the path include the top-secret base Area 51, Fort Knox and many others. Sacred Native American sites occur along the paranormal highway, mostly in the West, but not exclusively. Ancient civilizations, artifacts and burial mounds are associated with Mesa Verde National Park in Colorado, Zion National Park in Utah, Canyonlands National Park in Utah, Moab in Utah, Monument Valley Navajo Tribal Park in Utah, Comanche National

Grassland in Colorado, Cimarron National Grassland in Kansas, Chaco Culture National Historical Park (San Juan Basin) in New Mexico, Ancient Bristlecone Pine Forest in California and Cahokia Mounds in Illinois.

Animal mutilations occur along this stretch. Thousands of cows and horses have been found mysteriously drained of their blood. Reproductive organs, tongues and ears are removed with eerie surgical accuracy, leaving cauterized wounds. Oddly, the earth surrounding the gruesome scenes is left completely undisturbed, as if the mutilated animal was dropped from the sky.

Whatever the source of heightened paranormal phenomena and creativity, the enchanted Arkansas Ozarks sit smack dab in the middle of it. With this in mind, let's explore some of the anomalies and curiosities of the Ozarks.

Chapter 8
ARKANSAS HERITAGE

Perhaps the mystique of the Natural State is contained in its geological history that has morphed the land into hills and valleys where natural springs bubble through rock. No doubt it sits smack in the middle of natural beauty and discernable phenomena, and that draws certain people to experience the inexplicable. The first residents known to inhabit Arkansas were an assortment of native Indian tribes. Caddo settled in southwest Arkansas. Osage were in the northwest section of Arkansas and extended into Missouri.

The Arkansas state name derives from the Quapaw Indians and was known as South Wind by other tribes. The state with many nicknames is known as the Natural State, Land of Opportunity, the Bear State and the Wonder State. Unique to Arkansas, the wild frontier spirit of the West melds with the well-mannered spirit of the Old South like nowhere else.

Arkansas is bordered by Missouri to the north; Tennessee to the east, where the Mississippi River forms the border that divides the states; Louisiana to the south; and Oklahoma and Texas to the west. Of the six regions of Arkansas, this book covers the western portion of the state from north to south: Ozark Mountains, Arkansas River Valley, Quachita Mountains and Coastal Plain.

While the Ozark and Quachita Mountains are referred to as the Ozarks in general, they are not the same thing. The Ozark Mountains are in the northwest corner of the state and extend into southern Missouri. The Arkansas River Valley divides the Ozark and Quachita Mountains. The Quachita Mountains are located south of the Ozark Mountains and Arkansas River Valley. They end at the Coastal Plain, which extends to the southern state border.

OSAGE LIFESTYLE

Among the original Arkansas tribes, the Osage Indians of northwest Arkansas, who lived along the Osage and Missouri Rivers, were first discovered in 1673 by French explorers. The Osages were identifiable in several ways. Males shaved their heads, leaving only a long tuft of hair on the crown or hair that extended from the forehead to the back of the neck. The type of scalp lock indicated the clan to which the male belonged. Osage males wore deerskin loincloths, leggings, moccasins and bearskin or buffalo hide robes for additional warmth. Warriors tattooed their chests and arms.

Osage Indian females kept their hair long. They wore clothing perfumed with columbine seed, such as deerskin dresses, leggings, moccasins and woven belts. Furs of ermine and puma were worn as special ceremonial garments, along with earrings, pendants and bracelets. Like the Osage males, the Osage women also decorated their bodies with tattoos.

According to Osage tradition, the tribe formed when Wakondah, the creative force of the universe, sent Sky People down to join with Earth People. Likewise, Osage communities were organized into sections of Sky People and Earth People.

Family groups, or clans, related through the males. Each clan had its own position in the village, and each clan had a representative in village counsels for Sky and Earth tribal divisions. Village roads ran east and west. The Sky People clan lived on the north side of the road. The Earth People clan lived on the south side. The two village leaders, Sky and Earth, lived in large houses on opposite sides near the village center. Groups of elders, known as Little Old Men, established rules for village life. To become a Little Old Man, males had to train from boyhood, passing through seven stages of increasing complexity to master sacred knowledge.

The Osages were seminomadic, meaning their livelihood was based on hunting, foraging and growing food. Seasonal movements of the Osage brought them into northwestern Arkansas throughout the eighteenth century. Hunts, organized by a council of elders, were held three times during the year: spring, summer and fall. The men hunted bison, deer, elk, bear and smaller game.

Within the tribe, responsibilities for survival were divided among the males and females. The women were responsible for butchering animals the men had hunted. They dried or smoked meats and prepared hides. In summer, the women gathered wild plants and tended gardens of corn, beans, squash and pumpkins. When they had surplus meat, hides or oil, they traded with other Indians or, later, Europeans. The Osages acquired guns and horses from Europeans during the eighteenth century, which enabled them to extend their territory and control the distribution of European goods to other tribes in the region.

Ceremonies marked significant events, such as hunting, war and peace, marriage, healing and mourning the dead. Along with carrying out ceremonial duties and elaborate preparations, participants wore special clothing and ornaments or painted elaborate designs on their bodies.

Osage lands in Arkansas and Missouri were taken by the U.S. government three times: in 1808, 1818 and 1825. An Osage reservation was established in southeastern Kansas, where about ten thousand Osages are listed on the tribal roll today.

OSAGE LEGEND

The Osage legend about their tribal symbol, the spider, follows.

In old times, Wazhazhe (Osage) walked the earth and trapped and hunted with hardwood bows and arrows. They used animal hides for clothing and shoes and fur wraps for warmth. From tall prairie grasses, willow and river cane, they wove mats used for shelter. They were well fed, with many crops to sustain them, but they needed direction.

They looked to the animal kingdom for a symbol as a guiding force to find their place as part of the earth. Other clans had already chosen their symbols: the swift deer, the majestic buffalo, the sharp-eyed eagle. The Osage thought the only things left were possum, coyote or skunk. The clan leader told them to search everywhere for an important life symbol.

One Osage runner was so busy searching for a life symbol under every bush and in every treetop that he didn't see the spider web stretched across the path and ran headlong into it. As he pulled the sticky web off his face and body, he asked the spider why he built his house over the trail and caused him to run into it.

In return, the spider asked what the runner was searching for that he couldn't see where he was going. When the runner answered that he was looking for a life symbol for the clan, a being to guide them, the spider asked to be their life symbol. The runner hid his laugh from the spider and asked why the spider thought he would be a good symbol of the mighty Osage.

The spider explained, "Where I am, I build my house. And where I build my house, all things come to it."

Understanding the wisdom of the spider's words, the runner returned to the clan to tell his people the important life symbol he had found, but they weren't accepting. Compared to other clan's life symbols, like buffalo, deer and the eagle, the spider seemed like a bad choice.

The runner reasoned that buffalo must wander the prairie in search of food and deer must spend his days hiding from the hunter. The eagle must roam the skies in search of prey. But the spider has few enemies and does not spend his days hiding. The spider builds his house in a good place, and all things come to him.

"Our people will be like the spider," said the runner. "No longer will we wander, but rather make our home in a sheltered valley where the rivers flow and the sun shines. We will live in this good place, and all things will come to us."

Caddo Lifestyle

The Caddo lived in several tribal groups in southwest Arkansas and nearby areas of Texas, Louisiana and Oklahoma from AD 1000 to about AD 1800. Around 1700, Spanish and French explorers discovered them as three allied groupings: the Kadohadacho on the great bend of the Red River, the Natchitoches in west Louisiana and the Hasinai in east Texas. The Cahinnio, allies of the Kadohadacho, lived along the Quachita River. Although each group was independent of the other, all shared languages and customs.

The Caddo world had many supernatural beings with varying degrees of importance and power. The supreme being, Ayo-Caddi-Aymay, was the sovereign. To ensure favorable relations between people and the supernatural beings and cycle of life, rituals were performed. These included ceremonies for springtime planting and after harvest, birth and death, housebuilding, war and other community events.

Caddo society was organized by households and clans. Social position and political roles were based on clan membership. Political leaders were a ranked set of offices. A priest, or *xinesi*, held the highest civil and religious position. Other leaders oversaw secular or sacred activities. Shamans (*connas*) treated illnesses.

Before trade clothing became common, men wore breechcloths and moccasins with deer and bison skins added in winter for warmth. Both men and women decorated their bodies with paint and tattoos. Deerskin shirts with color and beaded designs and fringes were sometimes worn by both sexes. Men had several hairstyles; the most common was short with a long braided or decorated lock.

Women wore deerskin or woven skirts. In warm weather, they went topless, and they wore skin wraps in winter. Women wore their hair long, braided or tied close to the head. They sometimes tattooed their faces, arms and torsos with elaborate designs.

The Caddo were sedentary farmers who grew corn, beans, pumpkins and squashes, watermelons, sunflowers and tobacco. The Caddo males were responsible for hunting game and holding civic and religious roles and were involved in warfare. They hunted bear, deer, small mammals and birds with bows (*bois d'arc*) made of Osage orange wood and stone- or bone-tipped arrows. They foraged nuts, berries, seeds and roots. Caddo women raised children, tended gardens, made food and clothing, prepared skins and wove mats.

Those living near saline marshes or springs made salt by boiling brine in large shallow pans and then used the salt with food and for trading. They also traded oil or lard, bois d'arc bows. animal skins and decorated pottery to other Indians and European settlers.

Communities consisted of widely dispersed households separated by garden plots and woodlots. Each household had dwellings and work areas that varied in size and shape (circular, conical, oval or rectangular) made of timber stuck vertically into the ground and roofed with thatch or bark.

An elevated corncrib, outdoor work platform and upright log mortar for pounding corn usually stood near the dwelling. Sleeping and storage platforms, baskets and supplies were kept inside near a central fireplace. Woven mats covered floors and benches and were important ritual items. Each community also had a religious building located on an earthen platform mound, where rituals were performed and sacred items kept.

The multilayered organization of Caddo society provided a way to interact with Europeans. When European travelers approached, they were met along the path by a contingent of greeters from the community and then escorted to the dwelling of the Caddo and seated in a place of honor. Here, community leaders shared with the Europeans tobacco from a calumet, an elaborately decorated pipe stem and bowl, which created a bond of friendship.

The Caddo traded with both France and Spain during the colonial era. However, the westward spread of American settlement eventually encroached on their domain by way of disease, competition and hostilities. The Quachita valley tribes left Arkansas shortly after AD 1700. The last Red River communities were abandoned in the late 1700s, and by the nineteenth century, most Caddo were in Texas and reservations in Indian Territory.

CADDO LEGEND

In the Caddo creation story, Caddo believe that men and animals were brothers and lived together below the ground. There came a time when their leader, a man named Neesh, meaning Moon, discovered the exit from a cave leading to the earth's surface. Nesh told everyone to follow him out of the cave into the new land. The tribe divided into groups, each with a leader and a drum. Neesh told the people to sing and beat their drums as they moved along. He warned them to never look back the way they had come.

When they reached the cave opening, an old man climbed out first, carrying fire and a pipe in one hand and a drum in the other. Next came his wife, bringing corn and pumpkin seeds. Then came more people and animals, but when Wolf climbed out, he turned around and looked back the way he had come. Because Wolf looked back, the opening to the cave closed, shutting the rest of the tribe and animals under the ground, where they remain.

Those who had come out into the world of light sat down and cried for their people trapped below in the world of darkness. Because their ancestors came out of the ground, Caddo call the Middle World *ina'*, meaning Mother, and believe that they return to it when they die.

IRISH AND NATIVE AMERICAN FAIRY LEGEND

Fairies are thought to be nonhuman immortal earth spirits with supernatural powers who occupy a limbo between earth and heaven. Fairy lore is universal, with different theories about how they originated. One is they are descendants of the children of Eve. Another is that they are fallen angels not evil enough to be dismissed from heaven but not good enough to stay. A third is that stories told in parables about fairies arose to explain misfortune and disaster. Another suggests they are spirits of the restless dead, and another that they are simply small human beings.

Fairies are tiny beings resembling humans, but with wings, and are only visible to clairvoyants. They have an affinity for nature, live in a timeless underground world and come out at night to dance, sing, travel and have fun or make mischief.

Most Native American tribes have what they call "little people" as fairy lore. The Caddo of Arkansas have their version of little people as well. In Caddo folklore, the Lost Elves are ghostly nocturnal creatures that haunt thickets and wilderness areas. They are the size of children and live inside hollow trees. People who become lost in the wilderness may be turned into Lost Elves.

The lore of a fairy ring is the same around the globe. The fairy ring is defined as a circle of inedible mushrooms or unusually colored grass and is thought to be a magical circle where fairies meet to sing and dance at night.

Irish lore states that if you run around the outside of the ring nine times on a full moon, you'll see the fairies and your wish will come true. To interfere with the fairy ring brings bad luck, and if a human is lured inside the ring, he or she can't escape unless pulled out by a human chain. Inside the ring, time is thought to be different. What seems like a couple of minutes could actually be days, months or years.

In Irish tradition, it brings very bad luck to interfere with a fairy path. Houses will be built with consideration of where a fairy path exists, and the Irish will not knowingly build in the path. Houses with unlucky reputations are referred to as "in the way," "in a contrary path" or "in a path." Lore regarding doors and fairy paths is common in Ireland and Europe. When a house happens to have been built on a fairy track, the doors on the front and back—or the windows if they are in line with the track—cannot be kept closed at night, for the fairies must be able to march through.

OZARK ENGLISH

A dialect called Ozark English is spoken in northwestern Arkansas and the southeastern Missouri Ozark Mountains. The dialect is a relative of the Scotch-Irish dialect spoken in the Appalachian Mountains, the result of Scotch-Irish migration from Appalachia to Arkansas beginning in the late 1830s.

Geographic location and consequent isolation of the Ozark Mountains allowed preservation of select archaic properties of the dialect spoken by Appalachian settlers, which fostered development of the dialect that set Ozark English apart from standard American English. Like its Appalachian cousin, Ozark English has been linked to stereotypes that depict mountain culture as backward.

However, scholars began linking Ozark English to older forms of English as early as the 1890s, noting similarities between Ozark speech and terms found in English literature from the Middle Ages, as well as Elizabethan and Shakespearean literary periods.

In the twentieth century, researchers studied language in remote communities in the Ozarks, documenting various archaic words and usages. Charles Morrow Wilson, a Fayetteville, Arkansas native, and Vance Randolph (author of *Ozark Folklore and Magic*), a seminal figure in Ozark folklore studies, were among the scholars studying Ozark English during this period.

Wilson spent time with residents of Hemmed-in-Holler (Newton County) during the Great Depression, when he found that people could swap talk and break bread with farmers of Chaucer's England and suffer few misunderstandings. Wilson recorded that an Ozarker "tarries" to pass time and "carries a budget on his back," just as Shakespeare's characters did.

Randolph published several works on the Ozark dialect, many of which appeared in revised forms in *Down in the Holler* (1953), a collaboration with George P. Wilson, which explores various aspects of Ozark English, including its pronunciation, grammar and vocabulary. Like Wilson, Randolph recorded instances in which Ozarker pronunciation reflects earlier English, such as *heerd, deef, bile, strenth, chimley* and *anyways*.

The strength of the Elizabethan influence appears to be more concentrated in remote areas. Assessments indicate the connection between the Ozark dialect and earlier forms of English during the early twentieth century. In 1988, researchers Donna Christian, Walt Wolfram and Nanjo Dube published a study of Ozark English as part of a larger project to enhance existing linguistic studies through a comparison of Ozark English and Appalachian English.

A fieldwork group led by Dube documented properties in Ozark English, including the completive *done*, *a-* prefixing, irregular verbs and aspects of subject-verb agreement. The team studied the completive *done* (as in "I *done* told you") and concluded it appears almost exclusively in speech of those over fifty years of age. *A-* prefixing occurs in front of verbs, such as "He just kept a-beggin' and a-cryin' and a-wantin' to come out." Again, researchers observed fewer instances in younger speakers. The goal is to assert the Elizabethan influences that exist in isolated communities within the region, while acknowledging the changes in the speech of younger Ozarkers.

Ozark English—once nurtured by the region's geographic location and isolation from outside influence—has today become a fusion of the old and new, a unique dialect born of a people's cultural history.

Chapter 9
OZARK FOLKLORE AND SUPERSTITIONS

Ozark lore and legend is a melding of Native American and Scotch-Irish influences, from weather signs to superstition, water witches to medicine, courtship and marriage to pregnancy and childbirth, ghost stories to Ozark witchcraft and even death and burial.

ANIMAL FOLKLORE

The Ozark Howler is a legendary creature purported to live in remote areas of Arkansas, Missouri, Texas and Oklahoma. It's described as a bear-sized creature whose cry is like the melding of a wolf's howl and elk's bugle. It is sometimes seen with horns, and its black shaggy hair covers a thick body supported by stocky legs.

COURTSHIP

Girls create love charms by tying little pieces of cloth to the branches of pawpaw or hawthorn trees. If a man hides a dried tongue of a turtle dove in a girl's cabin, she will fall madly in love with him. Putting salt in a fire for seven consecutive days will bring a lover home, as will placing shoes on the floor so that the toe of one will touch the middle of the other and then reciting, "When I my true love want to see, I put my shoes in the shape of a T."

DEATH OMEN

An unusual sound inside a clock predicts a relative or friend will die. A clock that hasn't run for a long time but then suddenly chimes on its own accord indicates the number of days, weeks or months until a death occurs in the house. It is believed that an Ozarker who hangs his boots against a wall will not live to wear them out.

FEATHER DEATH CROWN

The feather death crown, sometimes called an angel crown, is a swirl of feathers that forms in a feather pillow when someone dies on it. According to folklore, the crown is created precisely as the soul leaves the body, indicating the deceased was a good person and went directly to heaven. Like a vortex portal, the swirl of feathers is arranged in a clockwise circular pattern, with the quills all facing the same direction toward the center of the circle. Crowns can range in size but are usually about four inches in diameter and about two inches thick. The swirl of white feathers is dense and feels eerie to the touch.

The tradition likely stems from Irish folklore from Tennessee that came into Ozark legend as the Appalachian Irish moved westward into Arkansas during the nineteenth century. The legend is well rooted in Appalachian culture, and the Museum of Appalachia in Tennessee has a small display of angel crowns from the pillows of dead children.

Those who reject the notion of the feather death crown as a good sign are likely to believe it is an evil thing, a bad omen that must be destroyed by fire. Some hillfolk simply will not have a feather pillow in the house. But if a feather crown is found in the pillow of someone who is ill, the hex can be reversed if the crown is immediately destroyed by fire. Some hillfolk will routinely check all the pillows in their house for any suspicious lumps. The idea is that feather crowns grow very slowly over a period of several months.

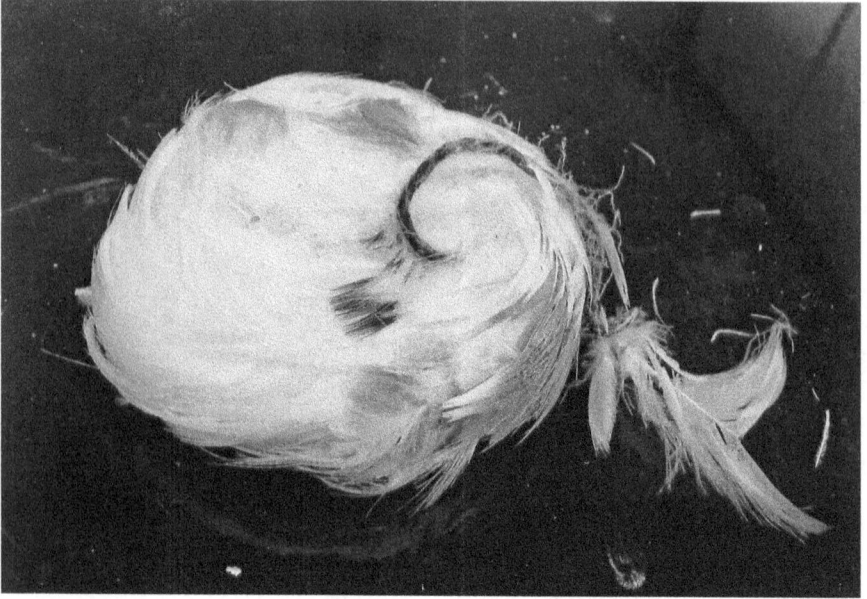

A feather death crown (circa 1918) with witch's ladder in core, property of author. *Author's collection.*

The hex can be stopped by searching the crowns out and burning them before they are completed. If not, the person who sleeps on that pillow will die. Some believe that's why you never find a perfect, finished crown, except in the pillow of someone who has died.

Whether the feather death crown is a work of God or a work of the Devil, it certainly can be considered an object of curiosity and worthy of its legend.

GHOSTS

A moth that lingers is the spirit of a grandparent. Ozark stories of hauntings fall into the category of the residual variety, where the spirit appears and repeats the same action over and over. With a residual haunting, the ghost doesn't seem aware of others, nor does it interact with the living.

MEDICINE

Hillfolk believe that unpleasant-tasting medicine is most efficient.

OZARK WITCHCRAFT

An Ozark witch is defined as a woman who bargains with the Devil for supernatural powers. The way in which a woman becomes a witch varies. One theory is that a woman becomes a witch if she fires a silver bullet at the moon and mutters obscenities. Another is if she fires seven silver bullets at the moon and repeats the Lord's Prayer backward.

PREGNANCY

Some believe if a pregnant woman crosses a running stream, she will die. A pregnant woman who "puts up" fruit will spoil the fruit. The sex of a child can be predetermined. For a boy, place a knife under the mattress. For a girl, place a skillet.

SUNDOG ATMOSPHERIC PHENOMENA

The sundog, also known as a mock sun, is a phantom sun that appears when sunlight is refracted through ice crystals in the atmosphere. Sundogs are seen during warm or cold weather. They appear to the left or right of the sun, or they appear as two phantom suns flanking the sun at the same altitude above the horizon. Sundogs and the accompanying rainbow halo that encircles the sun are most visible when the sun is near the horizon. Sundogs are difficult to photograph because their visibility is brief—just minutes before they fade and disappear. Native folklore claims that seeing a sundog during a journey indicates good luck.

WEATHER

Weather is predictable by omens and signs, depending on the hill or hollow, but no matter where you are when you see a tornado coming, run into a field and stick a knife into the ground with the edge of the blade facing toward the approaching funnel. The blade will split the wind and protect you from the funnel.

A tornado or severe storm is imminent if you see a hog looking at the sky when there is nothing there to attract its attention. When a hog carries wood in its mouth, a storm is coming.

A ring around the moon is a sign of bad weather. A blue line on the horizon at sunset predicts rain the next day. A rainbow in the evening means clear weather. But a rainbow in the morning means a storm within twenty-four hours.

A red sunset means twenty-four hours of dry weather. Lightning in a southern sky means dry weather, but seen in any other direction it indicates rain. If the leaves of a tree show their underside in a breeze, expect rain within a few hours. The size of the first raindrops indicates what kind of rain will follow. Small raindrops indicate rainy weather; large raindrops indicate a brief shower.

WATER WITCH

The sinister term *water witch* labels a waterfinder who has no association with the Devil and the practice has nothing to do with witchcraft; rather, it describes a person who searches for underground water using a dowsing rod.

Chapter 10

E. FAY JONES, TWENTIETH-CENTURY ARCHITECT

C onsidered a regionalist, Jones said during a 1944 radio interview, "I like to think of myself as being concerned with a higher order of things and probably the clearest manifestation we have of some higher order in the universe is what we see in nature and what we feel in nature."

BIOGRAPHY

E. Fay Jones (1921–2004) was born in Pine Bluff, Arkansas. His first name, Euine (pronounced *U-wan*), is an old Welsh form of *John*. He was the only surviving child in the family after two sisters died at early ages. The family stayed in Arkansas and lived in Little Rock and later El Dorado, where Jones earned the Boy Scouts of America rank of Eagle Scout.

His interest in architecture began in grammar school with designing treehouses. In high school, Jones decided to pursue a career in architecture after being inspired by a short film about the Johnson Wax Headquarters, designed by American architect Frank Lloyd Wright.

At the outbreak of World War II in 1939, Jones served in the U.S. Navy in the Pacific theater of operations as a naval aviator piloting torpedo and dive bombers. He married Mary Elizabeth Knox in 1943 in San Francisco, and they had two daughters.

EDUCATION AND FRANK LLOYD WRIGHT INFLUENCE

Jones began his education by studying engineering at the University of Arkansas in Fayetteville, where he was a brother of Kappa Sigma fraternity and graduated in 1950. He also attended Rice University in Houston on fellowship in 1949, which is where he met Frank Lloyd Wright at an American Institute of Architects convention.

They had an immediate rapport, and his affiliation with Frank Lloyd Wright became deep-rooted and long-standing. Their friendship picked up when Jones was teaching at the University of Oklahoma (1951–53) and Wright came there to present a lecture. Wright invited Jones to his winter workshop at Taliesin West in Arizona in 1953. Then in 1954, Jones spent the summer at Taliesin East in Wisconsin. Jones eventually became a Taliesin Fellow. Jones returned to the Ozark Mountains as a member of the faculty of the University of Arkansas School of Architecture and became its first dean.

The rural quiet of the Ozark Mountains, rather than urban landscape, influenced the architecture Jones designed. That kind of quiet in such a majestic environment should be experienced to understand why Jones chose the Ozarks over the glam of urban fame. In fact, he avoided urban trends and developed an organic aesthetic using materials found in the local Ozark environment, such as wood and stone. With his design of Thorncrown Chapel, Jones used construction materials that could be carried through the woods by just two men.

After he designed his own home in 1955, commissions in northwest Arkansas followed throughout the next two decades. His most renowned works are intimate spaces, chapels and private homes that transcend Frank Lloyd Wright's influence to touch on the human spirit. Although some of Jones's designs received national awards from the American Institute of Architects (AIA), it was not until Thorncrown Chapel in Eureka Springs was built (circa 1980) that Jones was widely recognized as a significant twentieth-century architect. Noted as one of the best designs of the 1980s by the AIA, Thorncrown Chapel harmonizes with its wooded environment where forest and sky transcend its glass walls. A stone floor, inspired by natural elements Frank Lloyd Wright often used, underscores the chapel.

THORNCROWN CHAPEL, EUREKA SPRINGS

The chapel is noted as one of the finest religious spaces of modern times. In addition to its many architectural design awards, it was also placed fourth on the AIA's list of the top buildings of the twentieth century.

Nestled in a woodland setting on sloping rocky terrain, Thorncrown Chapel is forty-eight feet tall. Its exterior walls contain over six thousand square feet of glass held in place by 425 windows, a genius design that fully integrates the chapel with the Ozark landscape.

E. Fay Jones labeled Thorncrown's style as "Ozark Gothic." The small chapel is twenty-four feet wide by sixty feet long and is constructed of pine two-by-fours, two-by-sixes and two-by-twelves, in harmony with its natural woodland setting. The Arkansas native's design plan mandated using building elements no larger than what two men could carry through the woods. Larger trusses were assembled on site and raised into place.

Thorncrown Chapel's ambience changes as shadow and light move through the space, constantly changing its tone throughout the day. In a broader sense, four distinct Ozark seasons and daily weather affect the mood of the glass chapel that takes on a life of its own throughout seasonal cycles.

Driving to Thorncrown Chapel on an Ozark mountain road involves navigating hairpin curves marked by the kinds of road signs you do not find in easy-breezy flat east Texas. Yellow triangles with snake-like symbols in no way prepare you for the reality of a curve with a stone bluff on one side of the two-lane road and a severe drop-off on the other.

At first impression, Thorncrown Chapel seems unassuming. The approach from the parking lot is along a stone path in the woods where the mountain continues to rise on one side. Like the road, the incline on the opposite side is a steep downhill drop. A small polite sign posted along the pathway states, "Please Stay on the Path."

Thorncrown Chapel exterior view approaching entry. *Author's collection.*

Thorncrown Chapel interior space. *Author's collection.*

When visiting Thorncrown, some tourists meander inside and stay just a few minutes. The true traveler will absorb the experience, taking as much time as desired. Visitors can contemplate their spirituality, consider the architecture or simply study a random spider that has taken up residence in the woods just outside the glass wall. A spider, as the spider in Osage folklore, lives by the credo "Where I am, I build my house. And where I build my house, all things come to it." This, from a seemingly insignificant creature that built a house on an acclaimed work of architecture. Sometimes truth really is stranger than fiction.

Just inside Thorncrown's double entry doors, visitors might notice a docent seated off to the left side. The sweet octogenarian stands and greets visitors and says time and again throughout the day, "This is a sit-down chapel. This is not a walk-around chapel."

Don't be fooled by her reserved demeanor; subtitles would read, "Sit your ass down." And regarding her ability to enforce the rules of the "Please Stay on the Path" signage, she is competent enough to chase you down if you stray off the path, and she will set you straight. Save yourself and stay on the path.

M.B. COOPER MEMORIAL CHAPEL, BELLA VISTA

The Cooper Memorial Chapel (circa 1988) is located in Bella Vista, along the paranormal highway, north of Bentonville and just south of the Missouri border. Augmented by Ozark Mountains of limestone and dolomite, Lake Norwood is situated beside the chapel. The chapel features glass windows and steel Gothic support arches that span the width of the chapel. The design recalls Frank Lloyd Wright's Prairie School of architecture and was praised as quietly commanding dignity and presence, uncommon among buildings of the era. The chapel is best described as a celebration of both God and His creation, according to the local people.

STONEFLOWER, HEBER SPRINGS

Stoneflower (circa 1965) is nestled among the southern Quachita Mountains and was added to the National Register of Historic Places in 2002. The residential structure appears to grow out of the stone landscape, hence the name Stoneflower. It features prominent design elements used by E. Fay Jones in Thorncrown Chapel in Eureka Springs and Cooper Chapel in Bella Vista. Stoneflower, built of salvaged boulders and wood, was inspired by the need to design a unique weekend cottage on a limited budget.

The home's entry at ground level is a cave-like garden room with natural rock walls, stone counters, tables and built-in sofa bases in the style of Frank Lloyd Wright. The main bathroom on the ground level re-creates a natural stone waterfall as its shower feature. A spiral staircase leads up to the next level, and the main living area features floor-to-ceiling windows spanning two levels, plus a cantilevered floating deck facing woodland rolling hills. Custom furniture and light fixtures designed by E. Fay Jones are a bonus. The upper level is an open-concept sleeping loft.

Chapter II

EUREKA SPRINGS

M ore than sixty highland natural springs gave birth to a thriving resort town where heavy mists frequently give the hills a mysterious ghostly visage, where water moves through rock, where sky quakes (thunder in clear skies) are common. At 1,260 feet in elevation, Eureka Springs, located on limestone, crescent-shaped West Mountain in the Ozark Mountains, is eight miles from the southern Missouri border at Leatherwood Creek, a branch of the White River. The town sits smack in the middle of the paranormal highway.

The year 1879 marks the beginning of Eureka Springs, destined to become one of the most popular health centers in the United States. Over a century's time, Eureka Springs became the artists' and writers' colony it is today, which features many art galleries, a writers' retreat and a shopping district comprising buildings in the National Register of Historic Places.

To qualify for listing in the National Register, a district must include a concentration of sites, buildings, structures or objects that are united historically or aesthetically by plan or physical development. The importance of a district lies in the collection of buildings that reflects the social and architectural history of the area. The five general categories for National Register of Historic Places properties are building, district, object, site and structure.

BASIN PARK HOTEL

Not only is the Basin Park Hotel listed in the National Register, and not only is it notoriously haunted, but it is also listed time and again in *Ripley's Believe It or Not!* The steep hills of Eureka Springs set the Victorian Basin Park Hotel apart as a wonder because every floor of the eight-story hotel backs against the mountain, inadvertently creating eight stories of ground-level entrances.

GROTTO

Eureka Springs lavishly augments its grotto with top-notch seasonal flower arrangements in large classic urns. Candles are kept burning inside the cave. Many visitors place written wishes in crevices formed by layered natural rock formation. Hand-crafted stone steps leading down to the grotto have carved identification marks, or symbols, that identify the mason who crafted it.

BLUE SPRING HERITAGE CENTER

Blue Spring Heritage comprises thirty-three acres of privately owned land that are open to the public daily during warm months. It features native plants and hardwood trees in a woodland setting and a natural spring that releases thirty-eight million gallons of water daily.

Now in the National Register of Historic Places for its archaeological significance as a site occupied between the Early Archaic and Mississippian periods, the heritage center is located at Highway 62 West, five miles west of Eureka Springs, Arkansas.

Historians from Tsalagi (Cherokee), Osage and Quapaw claim their tribes have lived intermittently at Blue Spring for tens of thousands of years. Excavated artifacts dated to between 8000 BC and AD 1500 prove the claim. As far back as ten thousand years ago, Native Americans, known as Bluff Dwellers, lived here and populated much of the Ozark Mountains. They were hunter-gatherers and traded goods with other tribes. It is noted that the Cherokee tribe made a stop at Blue Spring during the Trail of Tears in March 1839, when they were forced to march from Echota, Georgia.

CHRIST OF THE OZARKS

Christ of the Ozarks, circa 1965. *Author's sketch.*

Christ of the Ozarks is a monumental sculpture atop Magnetic Mountain overlooking Eureka Springs. Financed by Gerald L.K. Smith, creator and publisher of the monthly magazine *The Cross and the Flag* for racists and anti-Semites, the statue was sculpted by Emmet Sullivan, who also assisted at Mount Rushmore.

Christ of the Ozarks is a study in paradox in that it claims to be a minimal form, yet it stands seven stories tall. Dedicated in 1965, it weighs one thousand tons and towers at sixty-seven feet tall. Had it been seventy feet in height, an aircraft warning beacon would have been required to be mounted on its head. Reaction to this installation is mixed. While tourists are amused, residents have dubbed it as milk carton Jesus, Gumby Jesus or simply Jesus about to hang glide.

Continuing the paradox, note that when Gerald Smith died in 1976, he was buried at the base of *Christ of the Ozarks*. The super-right religious fanatic, whom critics referred to as Little Hitler, essentially created for himself a seven-story tombstone.

EUREKA SPRINGS CEMETERY

Eclectic Eureka Springs residents aren't limited to the living. Some are at peace in the Eureka Springs Cemetery high atop Magnetic Mountain. Ley lines run through this enchanting cemetery. Encountering one is an experience like no other. A tingling vibration enters the feet and moves up the legs, through the torso and arms and then through the neck and swirls out the top of the head in vortex fashion. Seriously. The sensation is that of renewal, not fear. A ley line runs alongside Annie Apple Van Marm's final resting place.

Annie was a Eureka Springs native and former stage dancer who toured with the Grateful Dead, and she is one of the eccentric people buried here. Her life ended in a tragic accident when she was just nineteen years old. Her grave is decorated with Deadhead memorabilia and colorful scarves like those she wore in life—that is, until a storm comes along and blows everything away. When that happens, people who visit start all over with the decorations.

Opposite Annie Apple Van Marm is the resting place of a Volkswagen bus–loving hippie. His tombstone is all done up in automobile metal shaped like a vintage VW bus. Painted on the back side are the words "On to the Next Great Adventure" and "Hippies must use the side door. No exceptions."

The hippie VW driver was born in 1965 and died in 2016. Annie was born in 1971 and died in 1991, which means they could have known each other in life. Is it possible that Annie hitched a ride in the afterlife, and they have gone on to the next great adventure? I like to think so, especially given the unmistakable magnetic ley line that runs between their two graves.

Stone bench, Eureka Springs Cemetery. *Author's collection.*

The grave of Annie Apple Van Marm, former stage dancer for the Grateful Dead, Eureka Springs Cemetery. *Author's collection.*

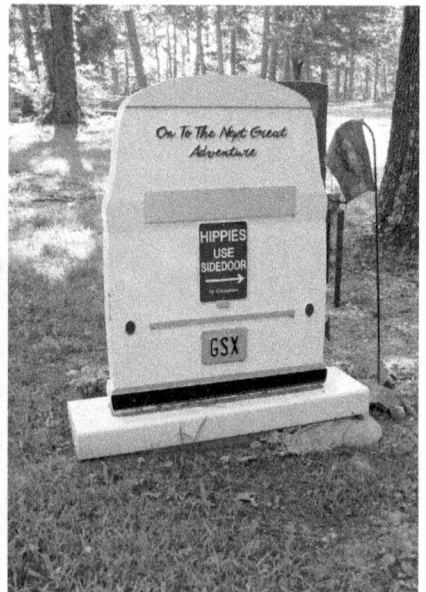

Volkswagen bus tombstone, Eureka Springs Cemetery. *Author's collection.*

For the visitor who likes to interact with local people, be on the lookout for the cemetery caretakers. They are a married couple who love to talk and tell stories to the extent that you won't doubt they could talk a dog off a meat truck. They are lovely people who will tell you about the cemetery and its spirit activity. For the brave of heart, ask about the very dark spirit they had to get rid of—but better not to ask how they did it.

MUD STREET CAFÉ

Where else in the world do you enter a building at street level and then walk down a flight of stairs to reach the first floor of an award-winning restaurant? At the Mud Street Café of Eureka Springs, Arkansas, of course!

You might wonder how this could be true. It turns out that there is a natural spring that runs underneath the circa 1888 building, which was originally constructed at street level. During the late 1800s, the spring kept flooding the street, thus the name Mud Street. The street has since been built up, putting the first floor down one level: underground.

The Mud Street Café dining room displays original local art and has unique features that include old limestone walls, large wooden beams, stained-glass lighting and a turn-of-the-century oak bar backed with beveled mirrors.

MUD STREET CAFÉ ANNEX

Where else can you eat breakfast and sip award-winning coffee while watching the water flow twenty feet below the very floor on which you are seated? The Mud Street Café Annex, of course!

Suspended over the forceful stream that gave "Mud Street" its name, the Mud Street Café Annex pays homage to the essence of Eureka Springs—the force of its natural spring water. The little sister annex of Mud Street Café, located at 28 South Main Street (next to the City Auditorium), will enchant you with its original tin ceiling, brick and limestone walls and repurposed wood bar. May the force be with you.

PIVOT ROCK PARK

Travelers have been touring the Pivot Rock Park roadside attraction in Eureka Springs for over one hundred years. The curious formation of layers of rock stands on its own power, like an inverted pyramid resembling a vortex. It goes without saying that almost everyone who visits has taken a classic pose standing a bit under the rock and touching it with one finger, giving the illusion of holding up the rock with one finger.

How did Pivot Rock get like this, and how much longer will it last? It not only sits precariously near the edge of a steep slope, but all its weight rests on a small section. It looks like the whole thing could topple over any minute.

Local Ozark legend Jesse James and his gang of notorious outlaws called the park home at one time. The truth is, if you listen long enough, you'll hear that most every place in the area claims to have been a James Gang hideout at some point.

Another geological oddity on the woodland slope is the Natural Bridge, which looks just like its name: a naturally occurring stone bridge. As natural bridges go, it's on the small side, but that works to the advantage of the visitor daring enough to walk over the arched rock surface. These geological anomalies make one entertain the notion that all this really was once an inland sea. It's easy to imagine seawater moving through and under the rock bridge and eroding the pivot rock in one fell swoop.

Classic roadside attractions like this were once a part of Ozark road trip culture: the gravity house, the mystery house, the many area caves and legends and other roadside attractions featuring, oh, say, two-headed snakes and taxidermized grizzly bears in attack stance.

QUIGLEY'S CASTLE, EUREKA SPRINGS' STRANGEST DWELLING

Italian Elise Fioravanti (1910–1984) came to the Ozarks when she was nine years old. She loved nature and the outdoors and began collecting rocks as a young girl during walks along an Ozark creek bed that led to her school. At age eighteen in 1928, she married Albert Quigley (1905–1972) during the Great Depression. When they moved to his farm and lumber mill, the rock collection accompanied them like one of the family.

Quigley's Castle, Eureka Springs. *Author's collection.*

Albert promised to build her a house with the lumber they cut from their own property. For fifteen years, they lived in a lumber shack and had five children. All the while, Elise Fioravanti Quigley imagined her dream house and often argued about it with Albert, who was reluctant to get started on it. Her patience began to wane.

Fifteen years after marrying Albert, Elise Quigley waited until he headed for work at the lumber mill one June morning in 1943 and then gathered their children around her and ordered them to help her tear down the three-room lumber shack. And so, they did. Albert came home that night to discover the house had been torn down and Elise had moved all their stuff into a chicken house. Albert might have wondered if they had a poltergeist.

Mrs. Quigley had already designed her dream home, including features she demanded rather than requested. She wanted lots of room for a robust family and a home where she felt like she was living in the outside world instead of in a wooden box. With her design in mind, Elise built her own architectural model using cardboard, matchsticks, scissors and paste.

Quigley's Castle, rock detail of exterior wall. *Author's collection.*

Garden art, vintage bottle tree.
Author's collection.

The biggest obstacle for Mr. Quigley, other than living in a chicken house, was to build the twenty-eight large windows Mrs. Quigley designed in the three-dimensional model, as glass was unavailable during the war. Let's just say he was motivated anyway and began construction immediately after moving into the chicken house. Mr. Quigley built the castle entirely out of lumber from their land, spending only $2,000 on supplies and glass.

Because the glass wasn't available for three years, the family survived brutal winters by tacking up material in layers over the windows, attempting to keep out the cold. Mrs. Quigley brought nature indoors by planting an indoor garden in the four-foot span of earth that was left bare, by design, inside the house. Mrs. Quigley planted flowering tropical plants that grew as high as the second-story ceiling. The plants are now over sixty-five years old.

Stones that she had collected as a young girl became an important feature of the house when Mrs. Quigley covered the outside walls with the collection of fossils, crystals, arrowheads and stone collected from creek beds. It took her three years to finish such a monumental task, but then she had

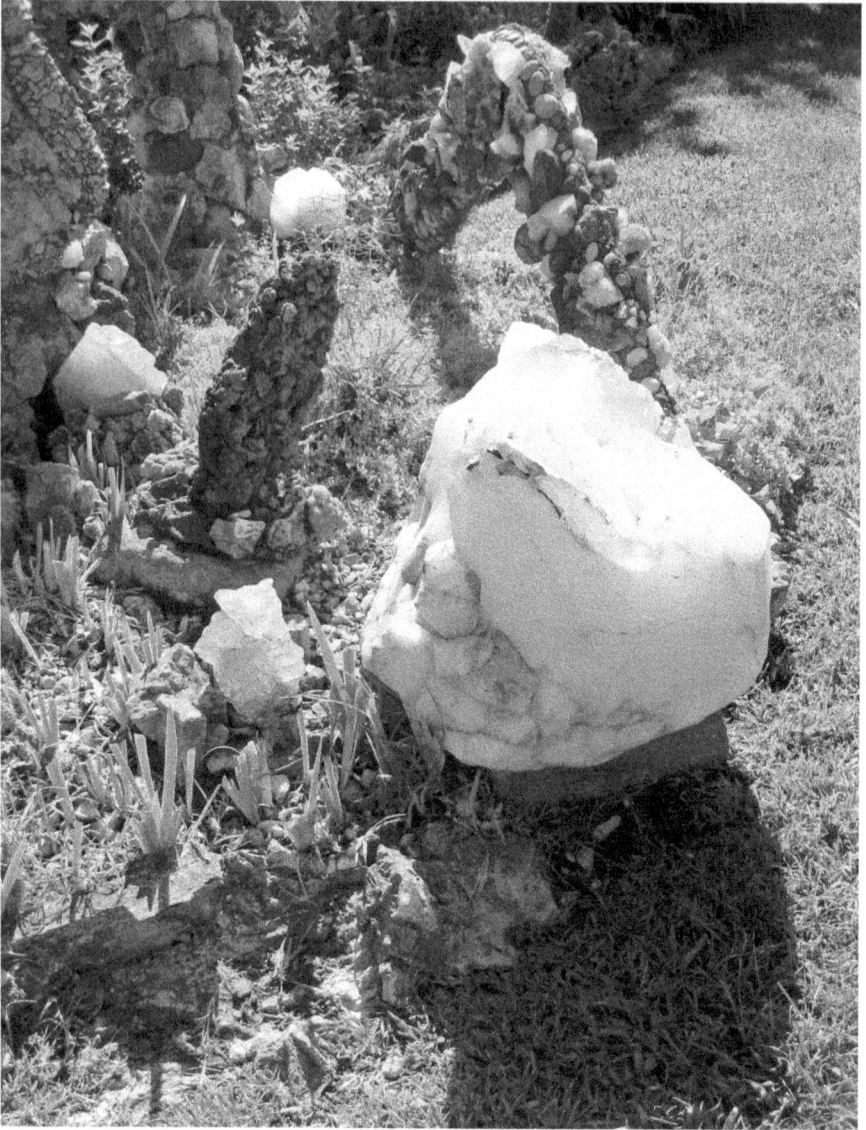

Garden art, large Arkansas quartz and creek bed rock art. *Author's collection.*

already waited fifteen years to have the house built. What was another three revolutions around the sun?

Mrs. Quigley was an avid gardener, with over four hundred types of flowers planted amid the garden sculptures she created with stones and whatnot.

ST. ELIZABETH OF HUNGARY
CATHOLIC CHURCH

Listed in *Ripley's Believe It or Not!*, St. Elizabeth of Hungary Catholic Church is the only church that you enter through the bell tower. St. Elizabeth was completed in 1906 with financial support by Richard Kerens, who also donated land for E.S. Carnegie Library on Spring Street, located between the Crescent Hotel and downtown Eureka Springs. Kerens also provided support for Thorncrown Chapel, designed by E. Fay Jones, the apprentice of Frank Lloyd Wright who returned to Arkansas and designed award-winning chapels that are located around the state.

Located on the sloping tier of mountainous land between the Carnegie Library and the Crescent Hotel, it is accessible and visible from the back side of the 1886 Crescent Hotel. From this vantage, orbs of light and other mysterious light anomalies have been photographed.

The path from the bell tower to the chapel entrance features the fourteen Stations of the Cross sculpted in white Italian marble. After sunset when the mountain is dark, the marble sculptures are illuminated and appear to

St. Elizabeth of Hungary Chapel, bell tower entry and Stations of the Cross. *Author's collection.*

Crescent Hotel with St. Elizabeth Catholic Church in the foreground, Eureka Springs. One-cent postage is required, which places it prior to 1952. *Author's vintage linen postcard.*

float in space. The Stations of the Cross is defined as a series of artistic representations, often sculptural, depicting Christ carrying the cross to his crucifixion in the final hours before he died. Devotions, or prayers, to honor the Passion are recited, sometimes with the worshiper moving physically around the set of stations.

EUREKA SPRINGS HAS A wide span of folklore. What with Osage Indians, the Dalton and James outlaw gangs sometimes hiding out in the woods and caves, Chicago mobsters from the Prohibition era making a ruckus, too many ghosts to count, UFO sightings galore, sky quakes among sixty natural springs on West Mountain alone and a cemetery high atop Magnetic Mountain where ley lines cross—the truth is sometimes stranger than fiction.

UFO CONFERENCE

Eureka Springs hosts an annual UFO conference each April; it is noted as one of the best UFO conferences in the country. The three-day convention features speakers who discuss UFO sightings and other related phenomena that include crop circles and alien abductions.

The annual conference was founded over three decades ago by Lou Farish (1937–2012), an understated man devoted to UFO history and research. Farish believed people see things all the time but rarely ever talk about what they see. He has been quoted as saying that no one thing drew him to study the UFO phenomenon, but he's been interested in the subject ever since he was dropped off by the mother ship several decades ago.

Whitley Strieber, author of the book *Communion*, has been a speaker at the conference. Strieber claims he was first abducted by aliens as he rode a train through Arkansas.

UNIQUE LODGING

Eureka Springs has no shortage of interesting vintage places for lodging, but for nontraditional travelers, check out the Eureka Springs Treehouses, Caves, Castles and Hobbits. You can get in touch with your inner cave woman or man, but private showing of the spaces is not an option before booking.

When visitors to Eureka Springs get a notion to sleep in a caboose or gas station (and who hasn't?), they can check out the Livingston Junction Cabooses, freestanding caboose hotel rooms featuring private decks and hot tubs. The Texas Bungalow is a popular repurposed vintage gas station. There are also log cabin lodges, grand turn-of-the-century haunted hotels and historic bed-and-breakfasts that range in style from cottages to mansions. Sherwood Court is an exceptionally clean vintage motor court. Your vehicle has its own little carport, and deer and fireflies come out at dusk in the woodland mountain setting. The outdoor firepit is a plus.

There are a few things to expect that are Ozark traditions, weird but desirable set in Ozark ambience. First: a heart-shaped jacuzzi tub is considered Ozark hoity-toity romantic. Do not be afraid when finding it in your bedroom. This is normal. It has not wandered out of the bathroom on its own power. Second: except for two Best Western Inns, there are no national chain hotels in Eureka Springs. Be strong. You will survive. Third: Ozark swimming pools are drained during the winter season. Visitors should note that although an empty pool looks like a *Caddy Shack* prank, it is not.

A path leading to a cave room at Eureka Springs Treehouses, Caves, Castles and Hobbits. *Courtesy of Eureka Springs Treehouses, Caves, Castles and Hobbits.*

The interior of a cave room. *Courtesy of Eureka Springs Treehouses, Caves, Castles and Hobbits.*

WIND CHIME

Eureka Springs is home to the world's largest tuned wind chime. The artist, Ranaga Farbiarz, created the chime noted in *Guinness World Records* at thirty-five feet, ten inches tall and weighing 653 pounds. Farbiarz dedicated the chime to his late father, Ignatz Farbiarz. Both of his parents emigrated from Poland to the United States in 1951, having survived the Holocaust.

WAR EAGLE MILL, ROGERS

In hindsight, it might be argued that War Eagle Mill can re-create itself no matter what. In several incarnations, it has been located on the same site since as early as 1832. The working gristmill has been destroyed three times and was last rebuilt in 1973. The mill currently operates as an undershot gristmill and houses a store and restaurant.

The first War Eagle Mill (circa 1832) was washed downstream in an 1848 flood. The second mill (circa 1860) prospered until the Civil War, when the Confederate army burned it in 1862 to prevent the Union from using it. The third mill (circa 1873) burned down in 1924. In its current iteration, the first and second stories house the mill and shop that sells grain products milled on site. The third floor houses a restaurant famous for cornbread, beans and ghostly sightings.

A Confederate soldier walks the banks of War Eagle Creek near the mill. Poltergeist activity is common in the restaurant, from kitchen noises to moving furniture and dispensers flying across the room.

The following history of the mill is printed word for word on paper packaging of a bag of cornmeal purchased from the mill in 2010.

In 1832, Sylvanus Blackburn left Tennessee with a wagon and four oxen, and came to the War Eagle River Valley in Arkansas. He spent the winter building a log home and clearing the land of his homestead. He brought his wife from Tennessee the next year. One of Sylvanus' first projects was a water powered grist mill. In 1848, a flood on the War Eagle destroyed the mill. A second mill, four stories tall, was soon erected. Five of Blackburn's sons joined the Confederate Army and the rest of the family went to Texas. The retreating Confederate Army burned the mill on War Eagle to prevent its use by Federal troops. Sylvanus' sixth son, James Austin Cameron

War Eagle Mill, a water-powered stone gristmill in Rogers. *Author's vintage linen postcard.*

Blackburn, built the third mill in 1873. The village of War Eagle grew around the grist mill. There was a sawmill, carpentry shop and blacksmith shop, but the grist mill was the center of activities—socializing, square dancing, and weddings. In 1924, once again, the mill burned. For nearly fifty years only the dam and raceway remained. In 1973, centennial year of the original mill, Jewell A. Leta Medlin and Zoe Medlin Caywood built the existing fourth mill on the same foundation as an authentic reproduction of the first mill to preserve the history of grist milling.

War Eagle Mill in Benton County is located at 11045 War Eagle Road, alongside War Eagle Creek. The mill is located approximately ten miles east of the city of Rogers in War Eagle, Arkansas, along the paranormal highway.

Chapter 12

1886 CRESCENT HOTEL

HOTEL HISTORY AND ARCHITECTURAL FEATURES

The entire town of Eureka Springs is said to be haunted by spirits from prehistoric times to the current day, with haunts spanning every era. Ghost tours feature hotel and Eureka Springs Cemetery spirits that span more than one hundred years of history. The 1886 Crescent Hotel was featured on *Ghost Hunters* in season 2, episode 13. With what they documented during one night of filming, the *Ghost Hunters* crew deemed the 1886 Crescent Hotel to be the holy grail of paranormal findings.

Eureka Springs became famous for its healing Ozark waters. People traveled to the remote location during the early 1900s seeking cures by way of spring waters said to heal aches and pains, as well as more serious ailments.

Designed by the architect Isaac L. Taylor, the 1886 Crescent Hotel was built by the Eureka Springs Improvement Company with help from the Frisco Railroad. It sits like a paranormal beacon on twenty-seven acres on West Mountain, a premium location with panoramic views of the valley and nearby hills. West Mountain is made of limestone and is crescent shaped—hence the name of the historic 1886 Crescent Hotel and Spa. The resort hotel and spa has seventy-eight rooms that host paying guests—and spirits that have been photo documented roaming the hallways and making appearances in guest rooms.

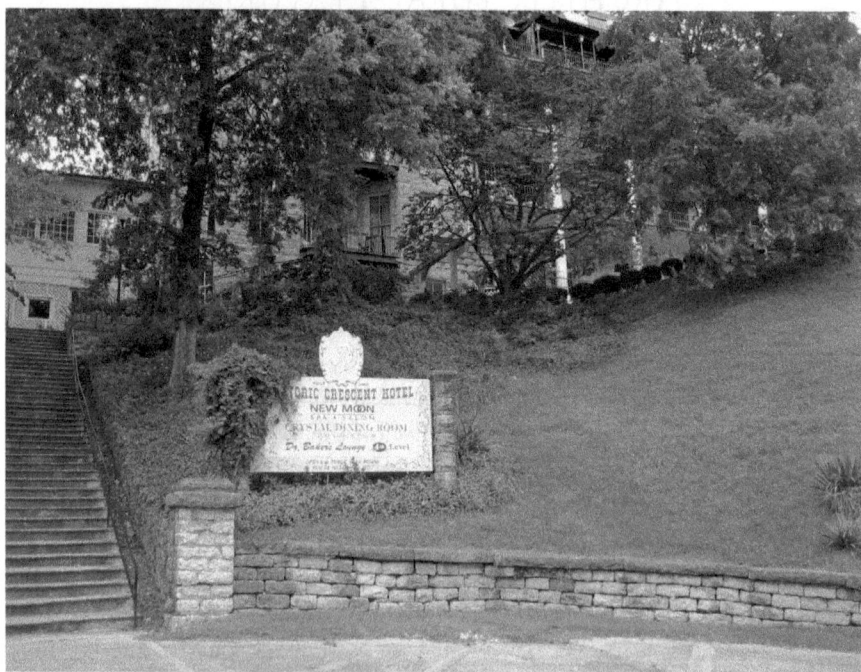

1886 Crescent Hotel, Eureka Springs. *Author's collection.*

The crescent moon marquee at the 1886 Crescent Hotel front entry leading to the lobby. *Author's collection.*

During the two years of construction, magnesium limestone was quarried on site at the White River and then crafted into eighteen-inch-thick walls that form an exterior mix of architectural styles. Towers, balconies and a wood-burning fireplace located in the lobby near the main entrance are among the hotel's features. The Crescent Hotel opened on May 20, 1886, with its lavish gardens in full bloom.

HISTORY OF THE 1886 CRESCENT HOTEL

The following information comes from the hotel's application for the National Register of Historic Places.

The 1886 Crescent Hotel is significant because it brought development to northwest Arkansas and the railroad to the Ozarks. It served as a refuge for the sick and weary, a vacation for the wealthy, a place of learning for the privileged. The region is now one of the most successful in the country.

1886 Crescent Hotel. *Vintage postcard.*

The 1886 Crescent Hotel and Spa is an architecturally significant work by world-renowned architect Isaac S. Taylor. A Nashville, Tennessee native, he graduated from St. Louis University with honors in classical languages. He was appointed chairman of the Architectural Commission and director of works for the World's Fair of 1904 in St. Louis. Other architecturally significant buildings Taylor designed in St. Louis include the Mercantile Club Building on Seventh and Locust, the Rialto Building on the southeast corner of Fourth and Olive and the Drummond Building at Fourth and Spruce. He also designed the original Union Station Hotel at the northwest corner of Nineteenth and Market in St. Louis, a building that shares architectural features with the Crescent Hotel, such as a rough-faced stone block exterior, Roman arches and a hipped roof with dormer windows.

The hotel's rough square stonework was crafted by masons who came from Ireland, using eighteen-inch stones quarried from ESIC quarry near Beaver, Arkansas. The quality of workmanship is so fine that the block walls were fitted without mortar.

The Crescent Hotel, a modern classic design, is a blend of French Renaissance and Richardsonian Romanesque styles, elements seen in Taylor's other works. It has concentric Romanesque arches above many of the windows of the first floor, along with stone walls and dormer windows. The five-story fortress was furnished with the latest Edison lamps and electric bells and featured a Waring sewage system and heat by steam through open grates.

The Crescent features a fireplace largely constructed of Eureka Springs' highly polished marble. Its unusual newel post and balustrade were completed out of native woods. At the foot of the main staircase, in the basement, were billiard rooms and a bowling alley under the promenade leading from the south porch. The building cost $294,000 to build in 1896.

Below is a brief history of the building and its occupants:

1902: The hotel was leased to the Frisco Railroad for five years.

1908: Crescent College opened and provided education to females until 1924.

1914: An advertisement in *Harper's Magazine* reads, "Crescent College and Conservatory for Woman. On top of the Ozarks. Famous for healthfulness and beauty of location. $300,000 fireproof building. Rooms with private bath. Elevator. Accredited Junior College. General Courses: Art, Music, Expression, Domestic Science. Address: Crescent College, Dept. H., Eureka Springs, Ark."

1937: Norman Baker purchased the hotel and remodeled it into the Baker Cancer Clinic. A charlatan by nature, claiming to have the cure for cancer, Baker made millions in today's dollars from cancer sufferers. However, it was his method of gaining patients that led to his undoing.

1940: Norman Baker was jailed for mail fraud. During his running of the Crescent, Baker equipped the hotel with an escape route from his first-floor office suite through a hidden staircase.

1946: The hotel saw a new round of renovations with four new owners: Herbert A. Byfield, John R. Constantine, Dwight O. Nichols and Herbert E. Shutter. Under new management, the hotel was restored, and travel vacation packages with the Frisco Railroad brought new tourists to the area.

1967: A fire that began in wiring claimed the penthouse level and most of the fourth floor.

1970: Dwight Nichols was the only living owner, and the hotel was turned over to Resort Enterprises Inc.

1972: The hotel was sold to Crescent Heights Developments Inc., owned by four investors: Dr. and Mrs. Sam H. Kouri and Mr. and Mrs. Robert Feagins. They restored the Crescent to its former glory, added modern amenities and expanded facilities in phases. It was during this period that supernatural occurrences were first reported.

1980: Riverview Management of Arkansas Inc. came in as a general partner.

1985: Willie Nelson played to a sold-out crowd in the Crystal Ballroom and then-governor Bill Clinton spoke at an annual chamber banquet.

1988: The Wichita Federal Savings and Loan of Wichita, Kansas, took possession of the hotel.

1997: Marty and Elise Roenigk purchased both the Crescent and the Basin Park Hotel. Announcing the dawn of the hotel's second golden era in 2000, the Roenigks said, "In five years, we will return the Crescent to where it was 100 years ago." Governor Mike Huckabee and his band Capital Offense headlined the celebration.

1997: Thirty-five guest rooms and New Moon Spa opened.

1999: The penthouse was properly restored, along with restoration of the original roofline and gardens. Rooms were refurbished so that all sixty-eight were complete.

2002: The annex became four Jacuzzi suites.

2004: The conservatory was rebuilt with a boardwalk and gazebo.

2007: Crescent Cottages was designed by architect David McKee, a former student of E. Fay Jones.

2019: An archaeological dig was underway regarding medicine bottles discovered buried on the property.

After Elise and Marty Roenigk bought the Crescent Hotel in 1997, it wasn't long before they called in certified mediums to "read the building." Carroll Heath and Ken Fugate, both of San Francisco and both certified mediums, were drawn to a section of the building at the outside annex above the morgue. Heath described it as a portal to the other side. During ghost tours, some visitors experienced physical symptoms at the location. They'd turn pale, slump against a wall and slide to the floor. To this day, the morgue is a hot spot of paranormal activity, likely going back to when the Crescent was used as a bogus cancer-healing hospital run by the charlatan Norman Baker.

However, the Baker years are only part of the building's history that accounts for its many hauntings. Let's explore some of the other possibilities. To read an updated account of visitors' paranormal experiences, check the ledger kept in the lobby for daily entries written by visitors, as well as the website.

ARCHAEOLOGICAL DIG AT THE CRESCENT HOTEL IS HISTORY IN THE MAKING, 2019

A project to extend the parking lot at the north end of the hotel's fifteen acres began in February 2019, but when a chance discovery seemed like a link to a chapter of the hotel's history, the work came to a sudden halt.

When Susan Benson, the Crescent Hotel's landscape gardener, began digging, she knew with the first scoop of dirt that something was amiss. What she happened upon turned out to be strange medical-looking bottles, a discovery that sent up red flags. Knowing the hotel's chapter as a bogus cancer-curing hospital run by the controversial Dr. Norman Baker during the 1930s, Benson called the hotel's ghost tour manager, Keith Scales, for consultation.

Scales recognized that the bottles were identical to those that appeared on an advertising poster of the late Norman Baker. More digging uncovered more glass bottles, one of which contained an unidentifiable object floating in a clear liquid—possibly a cancerous tumor Baker deviously claimed to cure, an image featured on a poster promoting the hospital.

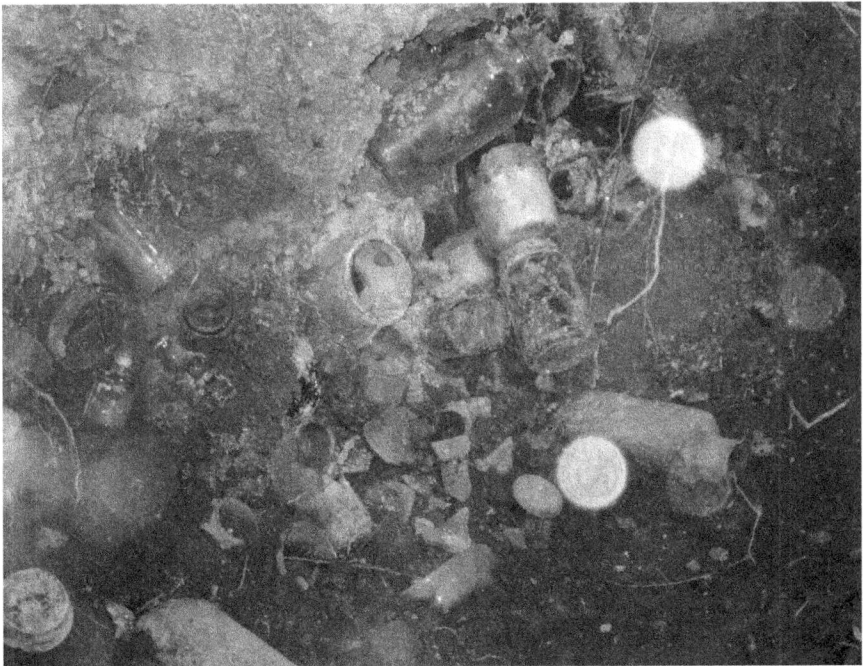

An archaeological dig site with orbs, Crescent Hotel. *Author's collection.*

An archaeological dig site showing excavated bottles with unknown contents, Crescent Hotel. *Author's collection.*

The hotel's general manager was called, and a "stop order" on any future digging was issued until University of Arkansas–Fayetteville archaeologists could examine the find. Their inspection led to involving the local police, who called the state crime lab and local fire department, who then brought in a hazmat crew.

Team members of the Arkansas Archeological Survey (AAS), part of the University of Arkansas system, arrived from the nearby Fayetteville campus to study the findings. They carefully removed layers of dirt and rock and cut through root clusters as more bottles were slowly uncovered.

With each descending layer of soil removed, AAS team members and hotel management hoped to find proof of the cancer hospital's history during the late 1930s. Baker had treated hundreds of patients who were desperate to be cured of terminal illnesses. There was no cure, only empty promises. However, Baker did extract millions of dollars from his patients, money scammed by way of mail fraud, which finally landed him in jail.

All the folklore and the hair-raising stories were proving to be true with each bottle unearthed. At least four hundred bottles have been found, and the excavation is far from over at this writing. The dig site is protected by a shelter built over it, but the VIP ghost tour includes a late-night romp through the dark woods with tour director Keith Scales leading visitors to the work in progress. Photographs are permitted, and sealed jars recovered from the dig are passed around the tour group for hands-on examination. Some contain specimens.

Apparitions of the destitute cancer victims and former nurses and hospital staff visit the hotel today. Baker has been seen in the hotel lobby dressed in a white linen suit and purple shirt.

DR. JOHN FREMONT ELLIS

The illustrious spirit of the hotel's former resident doctor, John Fremont Ellis (not to be confused with Norman Baker, the charlatan), resides in room 212. He smoked cherry pipe tobacco, and the scent is often sensed during ghost tours. One tour documented twenty-four people all smelling it at the same time for more than one minute.

GHOST TOURS

Many ghostly images are photo documented on the Crescent Hotel website by visitors to the hotel. Although the professional tour guides seamlessly weave the Crescent's historical background with its many hauntings, tours end with an eerie visit to the former morgue that is staged with an autopsy table and recently excavated medical bottles displayed on shelves behind protective glass doors. Visitors are shown film footage of a convincing *Ghost Hunters* episode (season 2, episode 13) when the hotel was deemed the holy grail for paranormal investigators. Footage taken with the heat-sensitive camera shows the defined image of a young man leaning against a locker and staring down the film crew. Given the reputation of the alluring Irish stonemason Michael, who fell to his death during construction of the building back in 1884 and now haunts room 218, the heat image of this young man could very well be him—brash and cocky and full of himself.

GIRL IN THE MIST, BALCONY HAUNT

The Girl in the Mist legend is a residual haunting, meaning the same haunting actions are repeated over and over again without deviation. The ghost has no awareness of nor interaction with the living. It is defined as the result of psi energy imprinted on the environment and replayed time and again endlessly.

Psi is the twenty-third letter of the Greek alphabet, and its energy is associated with psychic or paranormal phenomena. Additionally, psi operates outside the boundaries of space and time, and it is not affected by the laws of physics, thermodynamics or gravity. It doesn't require exchange of energy, nor is it governed by the laws of relativity, which holds that nothing can move faster than the speed of light.

Some paranormal theorists claim that the presence of quartz crystal can be a component to a residual haunting in that the crystal behaves as an energy source that captured the original event and plays it over and over, like a memory. With that in mind, consider the mountain where the 1886 Crescent Hotel resides: West Mountain, the crescent-shaped limestone mountain. The legend follows.

During the early 1930s, when the building was a conservatory for girls from wealthy families, legend has it that a young student fell to her death from the west veranda third-floor balcony. She reappears over and over again as a mist. Some claim the mist is the girl, while others claim to see her inside the mist. Either way, the mist repeats the fall from the third-story balcony endlessly, as if in a time loop.

Her name has been lost to time and the ensuing family scandal suppressed, but the legend remains. Questions arise with the legend. Did she jump? Was she pushed? Or is there another option that involves the figure of a man seen in the shadows of the balcony as the ghostly mist falls? Some conjecture that she was with child and the man denied responsibility when she told him he was the father. Based on movement by the shadowy man, some claim he tried to save her from jumping, that he grabbed her but lost his grip and she fell to her death.

GUEST ROOM HAUNTS

Guests have experienced lights and the bathtub water spigot turning themselves on, a refrigerator unplugging itself and personal items that go missing only to be found in obvious places. Guests experience pokes in the behind and the phenomenon known as the psychic staring effect, where humans detect (by extrasensory means) that they are being stared at. Doors open or close of their own accord. Spectral images have been seen looking back at the visitor from inside mirrors, and some sense an occasional unknown presence sitting on their bed.

DINING ROOM AND KITCHEN HAUNTS

The hotel's Crystal Dining Room has frequent paranormal activity. Here, Victorian-dressed apparitions have appeared. Visitors have seen groups of 1890s dancers, in full-dress attire, whirling around the room in the wee hours of the morning. Others tell of a nineteenth-century gentleman sitting at a table near the windows. When approached, he says, "I saw the most beautiful woman here last night, and I am waiting for her to return."

A former waitress reported seeing the image of a Victorian bride and groom in the dining room's huge mirror. When the groom made eye contact with the waitress, he faded away.

Victorian spirits that linger in the dining room are mischievous and playful. During the Christmas season, a decorated Christmas tree and its packages were found mysteriously moved to the opposite side of the room, and all the chairs were arranged in one big circle facing the tree.

In the kitchen, the apparition of a small boy has been seen skipping around, and sometimes pots and pans come flying off their hooks of their own accord.

HALLWAY HAUNTS

A nurse pushing a gurney that resided in Dr. Baker's morgue has been seen guiding the squeaky, rattling gurney down the halls of the hotel. A ghostly waiter has been seen in the hallway carrying a tray of butter.

Lady in White, Garden and Balcony Haunt

The Lady in White is seen wearing a flowing white gown. At about four feet tall, she floats through the gardens and perches on balconies.

Lobby Haunts

In the lobby, a gentleman dressed in formal Victorian clothing, complete with top hat, has been spotted sitting at the bar at the bottom of the staircase. Described as distinguished looking, he has a mustache and beard. Many visitors have attempted to entice him into conversation. He sits quietly and doesn't respond, then suddenly disappears. Cherry pipe tobacco often wafts through the lobby area, and Morris the Cat makes appearances here, as well.

Michael, the Irish Stonemason, Room 218

Room 218. Michael's room has the most paranormal activity in the hotel and is the most requested. *Author's collection.*

The most talked about haunt is a red-haired Irish stonemason known as Michael, a reputedly handsome young man who posthumously earned the reputation as a prankster and self-assured flirt. He arrived in Eureka Springs from Ireland in 1884, one of a team of stonemasons employed to work on the building that would eventually house the Crescent Hotel.

Michael's demise came while working on the roof of the Crescent Hotel when he lost his balance and fell to the second floor. The area where he landed now houses room 218, known as the guest room with the most paranormal activity. It is the most requested room as well.

Michael is evidently a mischievous spirit who likes to play tricks by turning the lights in room 218 off and on, opening and closing doors and turning the television off and on. He also pounds loudly on the walls. Some guests have heard loud cracking sounds, like wood splitting, coming from the bed's headboard and footboard. Others have witnessed hands coming out of the bathroom mirror and heard cries coming from the ceiling—cries that sounded like a man falling. Could the male image captured on film by *Ghost Hunters* researchers be the image of Michael? Some believe it is.

MISS THEODORA, ROOM 419

Theodora lived at the hotel from 1937 to 1940 during Norman Baker's cancer-curing hospital run. Her room 419 residence, where doors open and close on their own, is known as not scary but damn interesting. The older woman has been seen in the hallway dressed in a nurse's uniform, fumbling for keys at the door to her room. Theodora has the reputation for preferring older guests. She dislikes guests who are disharmonious. Preferring peace, she's known to repack bags of bickering or untidy guests when they leave the room for dinner. Upon returning, they find their bags packed and placed by the door, Theodora's obvious suggestion to leave.

Room 419, Miss Theodora's room, showing a faint orb on the door. *Author's collection.*

One story told on the ghost tour involves Theodora and a bickering couple who planned their wedding at the Crescent Hotel for the following day. Amid bickering, they hung their wedding clothes in the closet and then left the room to go to dinner. Upon their return, they found the wedding garb strewn on the floor and their bags packed and waiting at the door.

A story was told during a 2008 ghost tour led by guide Carroll Heath regarding Theodora's appearance when the hotel hosted a paranormal investigation. Theodora appeared to Heath, a psychic and certified medium, and complained about what she described as a "silver book." Apparently, she developed a loathing for silver laptop computers, which she associated with all the hoopla of an investigation.

MORGUE HAUNTS

A hotel maintenance man witnessed all the washers and dryers mysteriously turn on in the middle of the night in the laundry room located next to the former morgue.

Morris the Cat, known as the former hotel mascot, makes his presence known in the morgue.

While investigators were filming an episode of *Ghost Hunters* (season 2, episode 13), thermal cameras picked up the image of a male figure staring them down while leaning up against locker #2. Not only did the thermal camera clearly define the male figure, but it also indicated the metal locker's #2 as being warm, as if heated by the apparition leaning up against it.

MORRIS THE CAT, A FELINE HAUNT

When visiting the Crescent Hotel, don't be alarmed to feel a ghost cat jump on your lap or brush up against your legs. It's just Morris, the resident feline ghost.

Among the hotel's many tales of hauntings, Morris headlines the list of favorites. The orange tabby, named after Morris the Cat of the 9Lives cat food fame, was the hotel mascot from 1973 to 1974. Like his namesake, Morris the mascot was smart and independent. Not only did Morris have his own private pet door entrance, but he also had his own little flat.

His commanding presence earned him the nickname General Manager by hotel staff. At Morris's passing, the hotel management held a well-attended wake for him. Morris's portrait hangs in the hotel lobby, along with a memorial plaque and a poem about the cat. Morris is buried in a flowerbed just beyond the veranda in the back of the hotel.

Eureka Springs resident Rebecca J. Becker, a local artist who painted ghost portraits that now hang in the Crescent Hotel's hallways, has experienced spectral Morris. While sketching in the lobby, Rebecca felt a cat jump up in her lap only to discover there was nothing there. It's common for ghost tour guests to feel the feline resident ghost brush up against their legs in the morgue during a tour.

SWITCHBOARD HAUNT

For a time after the hotel updated phone equipment and discontinued using the original outmoded switchboard, it continued to receive calls from the otherwise empty basement. This led to permanently disconnecting the switchboard.

As a side note, it is not uncommon for spirits to contact the living through telephones. People who have lost loved ones sometimes receive calls showing the deceased's name on the caller ID display, long after their phone was disconnected. When the call is answered, there is usually only static on the line; however, sometimes the deceased will deliver a message. The author Dean Koontz received a warning message via telephone call from his deceased mother. Some have received chat requests on social media from the deceased.

Chapter 13

BENTONVILLE AND FAYETTEVILLE

BENTONVILLE

Bentonville's history reads like a fairytale that begins with Indian folklore, spans pioneer settlement and the Civil War era, transcends agriculture and industry and then morphs into a celebrated art mecca and home to the world-class Crystal Bridges Museum of American Art.

The Missouri Osage tribe hunted this Arkansas land before settlers arrived. Scottish and Irish settlers arrived and established farms and renamed the Osage colony Bentonville in honor of Thomas Hart Benton, a Missouri senator. Cherokee people passed through during the Trail of Tears in 1836 on the path to Indian Territory. Post–Civil War buildings, rebuilt during the Reconstruction era, now stand as the oldest historic structures in Bentonville.

Benton County became the leading apple-producing county in the nation and a leader in poultry production all before Sam Walton opened Walton's 5 and 10 Variety Store in 1951, which morphed into Walmart, the world's largest retailer.

Crystal Bridges Museum of American Art

The travel guide *See the USA the Easy Way: 136 Loop Tours to 1200 Great Places*, published by Reader's Digest in 1995, doesn't even mention Bentonville, Arkansas. Yet by the time Crystal Bridges Museum of American Art opened in 2011, Bentonville was unexpectedly on its way to becoming a celebrated mecca of fine art, as if out of the clear blue sky.

Bentonville took the world by surprise, thanks to the vision of Alice Walton, daughter of Walmart founder Sam Walton, who spearheaded the foundation's involvement in developing Crystal Bridges Museum of American Art. Admission to the world-class museum is free to the public.

Designed by architect Moshe Safdie and engineer Buro Happold, the museum's glass-and-wood construction features a series of pavilions that echo the crystal form. Pavilions are constructed around two spring-fed ponds, where forest trails meander among the soil that is flinty silt loam derived from chert and cherty limestone. The 217,000-square-foot complex includes galleries, meeting and classroom spaces, a library, a sculpture garden, a museum store and a restaurant and coffee bar. Extensive nature trails encircle the wooded museum campus, augmented by outdoor installations that include an authentic Frank Lloyd Wright house, James Turrell's Skyspace, recently acquired Dale Chihuly glass installations and traveling exhibits.

You enter the museum via an elevator that transports visitors down one story. When the elevator doors open at ground level, visitors exit into the courtyard entry, which is enveloped by a Louise Bourgeois two-story spider sculpture, *Maman*, circa 1999. Marble orbs representing spider eggs are contained within the underbody of the spider. To the sculptor, the spider represents the mother figure, yet it is in perfect harmony with the Caddo legend of the spider's wisdom as their life symbol. The spider explained, "Where I am, I build my house. And where I build my house, all things come to it."

The artist Louise Bourgeois compared the spider to her mother, a tapestry woman, and called it subtle, indispensable, neat and useful. Bourgeois welcomed spiders into her home as small heroines to rid her of mosquitoes and admired the connection conveyed by their webs. Believed to be 300 million years old, the spider embodies the ancient soul of existence reverberating creativity and predation. Nature has made the spider a most uncanny being, a trapeze artist dangling from its silken thread and reeling itself up again, a spinner of virtuosity, a cunning hunter with a wide net.

James Turrell's *The Way of Color* is a site-specific work of installation art on the Crystal Bridges campus. It is one of Turrell's many Skyspaces and features a domed ceiling with an oculus opening directly to the sky. A series of LED lights illuminates the dome's interior, and as the lighting sequence runs its course, that framed glimpse of evening sky seems to shift dramatically in hue, well beyond what you usually see at sunset.

Maman, circa 1999, Louise Bourgeois, at the main entry to Crystal Bridges Museum of American Art. *Author's collection.*

A rare Frank Lloyd Wright house on premises is of the Usonian style, which was developed as an affordable house for average people. The museum house, known as the Bachman-Wilson House, was originally built in the borough of Millstone, Somerset County, New Jersey, in 1954. Because the Millstone River encroachment endangered the house, the museum was able to purchase and move it to the current location. Tours of the house interior are free and self-guided, but a timed ticket is required. The Bachman-Wilson is worthy as a destination, yet its significance is compounded because Frank Lloyd Wright mentored the Arkansas architect E. Fay Jones, whose chapels are in nearby Eureka Springs and Bella Vista.

Newly acquisitioned glass sculptures by Dale Chihuly are on exhibit throughout the museum buildings and outdoor exhibition spaces.

Categorically, the museum's collection consists of prints, photographs, paintings, watercolors, sculpture, drawings, mixed media, decorative arts and textiles. Like no other museum, Crystal Bridges Museum of American

The Way of Color, circa 2009, James Turrell. *Author's collection.*

Bachman-Wilson House, circa 1954, Frank Lloyd Wright, Usonian design. It was endangered by river encroachment and moved to Crystal Bridges Museum from Somerset County, New Jersey. *Author's collection.*

Bachman-Wilson House, side view. *Author's collection.*

Turquoise Reeds and Ozark Fiori, circa 2012, Dale Chihuly. *Author's collection.*

Left: *Azure Icicle Chandelier*, circa 2016, Dale Chihuly. *Author's collection.*

Below: Unknown title, floating glass spheres, Dale Chihuly. *Author's collection.*

Art is a masterful integration of Arkansas's natural landscape with the museum's architecture and fine art collection. Included in the collection is a 1,500-pound crystal cluster that was mined near Jessieville, Arkansas. It is estimated to be 350 billion years old.

The museum invokes a sense of connection to our American history, as expressed uniquely through American artists from colonial times to the present day. A visit to Crystal Bridges is a spiritual encounter, amplified by mystical geological elements.

Bentonville Haunts

One of the most popular Bentonville haunted spots is the Station Café, a former theater noted for items moving around in the dining room and kitchen of their own accord and a male apparition that roams the hallway. The haunted café is located at 111 North Main Street.

The Historic Peel Mansion, listed in the National Register of Historic Places in 1995, is a fourteen-room, circa 1875 villa tower Italianate mansion and is haunted by Colonel Samuel West Peel and his daughter Minnie Bell. The colonel's ghost has been seen in the kitchen, and staff have reported the sound of a piano playing in the parlor even though there's nobody in the room. Minnie Bell was known to play piano in that room when she was alive. An apparition of a woman in white has been seen, and disembodied cries are heard in an upstairs bedroom. Visitors have been pinched by unseen fingers while touring the second floor. The two-story stucco brick masonry structure is located at 400 South Walton Boulevard in Bentonville.

Nearby, a phantom horse and rider have been seen on Radar Road at the outskirts of Rogers.

Museum of Native American History

The Museum of Native American History in Bentonville, according to its website, invites the visitor to discover fourteen thousand years of indigenous history by exploring one of North America's most important museums dedicated to the peoples of the Americas. The permanent collection of the museum explores five distinct periods of human existence in the Americas, organized chronologically and spanning from fourteen thousand years ago to the early days of European influence. The museum invites the visitor to be captivated by the history of indigenous peoples of Arkansas and stand face to face with a woolly mammoth skeleton.

The Arkansas museum's broad scope explores the history of all Native Americans rather than a single tribe, displaying a vast collection of weaponry, arts and crafts and archaeological artifacts. You can self-guide with an audio wand. Stops at museum highlights include the Sweetwater Biface, noted as one of the thinnest flints discovered in North America, and the Gunther points discovered in California and southern Oregon. The museum's weaponry collection includes delicate bows and arrows alongside war clubs used in battles.

A large collection of handicrafts and traditional art is a highlight of the museum. Meso-American ceramics, including human effigies, are grouped alongside Mimbres pottery. A collection of Mississippian pots shaped like human heads are considered the rarest ceramics in the museum.

Admission and audio guides are free. The museum is located at 202 Southwest O Street in Bentonville.

FAYETTEVILLE

Located on the northwest outskirts of the Boston Mountains, a subset of the Ozarks, Fayetteville has long been known for its innovative spirit. It's an academic center nicknamed the "Athens of the Ozarks," with rolling hills and architecture listed in the National Register of Historic Districts. Fayetteville has been home to the University of Arkansas since its 1871 founding. It's where we enter the realm of the paranormal highway at the thirty-sixth parallel.

Fayetteville Haunts

Fayetteville Confederate Cemetery is allegedly haunted by ghosts from the Battle of Pea Ridge and Prairie Grove, circa 1862. Although many men died in battle, most perished from the winter storms and disease-ridden camps. Ghostly echoes of rifle shots have been reported, as well as glimpses of diseased and frostbitten soldiers. The biggest Civil War battle fought west of the Mississippi was at Pea Ridge Military Park, just north of Rogers. The 1862 battle between Union troops and a Rebel force that included local Cherokees prevented the Confederates from invading Missouri and capturing St. Louis. Fayetteville Confederate Cemetery is located at 14 East Rock Street.

Fayetteville Healer

A retired couple checked into the Homewood Suites in Fayetteville. Although the woman was slowly recovering from a pulled hamstring in the left leg, they were headed to Bentonville's Crystal Bridges Museum of American Art to see a traveling exhibit that was nearing the end of its run. After a long day's drive that began in Texas, Fayetteville was a good stopover. After a good night's rest, the couple headed downstairs to the dining room for breakfast, where the woman secured a table and waited for her husband.

A young man approached the table and asked, "Are you in pain?"

Wide eyed with surprise as her husband approached the table, she said, "Well, as a matter of fact, I am."

"Is it your right leg?" asked the young man.

"No, it's the left. I pulled a hamstring," she said apologetically, curious as to how the man was on to her painful injury, albeit he was slightly off but close enough to arouse her curiosity. The necklace she wore might have tipped him off, what with the artisan-crafted silver crescent moon and companion quartz crystal strung together on a simple jewelry chain. Whether injured or not, she wore the favored necklace just about every day in an oh-so-Stevie-Nicks way.

"I'd like to pray for God to heal you. Is that OK?" asked the young man.

She imagined a prayer chain or her name in the local church bulletin, and so she agreed.

The encounter turned the corner to Wacky Street when the young man unexpectedly went down on his knees next to her at the table. He placed his hand over hers, closed his eyes and bowed his head.

The couple exchanged curious glances, interested to see where this adventure would go. The young man offered up a prayer for healing to Almighty God, the Creator of the Universe. With what might be considered an attitude in polite company, the young man demanded that God remove the pain.

Once again, the couple exchanged glances, as their previously pleasant facial expressions began to gather storm clouds.

"Are you still in pain?" the young man asked afterward, asserting confidence.

"Well, yes, I'm still in pain," she said to a very surprised self-declared healer. Apparently, this guy was used to getting his way by verbally assaulting the Higher Power.

"Well, then we need to do it again," and so once again he commanded the Creator of the Universe to take away the pain, and once again the couple exchanged glances. This need for a second request transcended the previous and knocked everyone within hearing distance into new territory.

"Are you in pain now?" he asked for the second time.

Frankly, she didn't want to disappoint. However, reality prevailed with the plus-sized woman sitting on a hard chair and most definitely suffering pain that accompanies a pulled hamstring, an injury caused when the woman fell and essentially did the splits. For all intents and purposes, the healer might have demanded a new body. The antagonist in her wanted to ask him why God didn't prevent her from falling in the first place.

"Well, um, yes, I am still having pain," she said.

"We need to pray again," he said, serious as a heart attack.

The couple locked eyes, eyebrows raised. On the one hand, they each wanted this to play out because it was becoming humorous. On the other hand...

"No, this is getting to be too much. No more, this is my wife," said the husband.

The young man went his way, and the couple headed northbound toward Crystal Bridges and the Chihuly glass exhibit. They spent the entire day exploring the museum and its campus and then headed back to Fayetteville's Homewood Suites for another night's stay.

The next morning at 7:00 a.m., they awoke to one rude fire alarm. Helen Keller could not have slept through the noise and flashing lights. With no smoke or burning smell, the couple hastily packed bags and headed down four flights of stairs, the woman on an injured leg. In a twist of irony, the young healer met them head-on as he ascended the stairs and passed by without even a nod of recognition.

"Well, that's rude," the woman murmured under her breath. "He knows I'm in pain. He might have offered to carry my bag down the stairs."

Terra Studios

Fayetteville is also home to Terra Studios, where artsy locals are dedicated to the arts and to inspiration, education and creativity, and they aim to create a better world through art. The grounds of Terra Studios showcase a labyrinth and woodland pathways featuring fairies and gnomes. The gift shop is an explosion of sculpture, jewelry and pottery. Terra Studios is home to the blue glass Bluebird of Happiness. There is something here for every age group.

Terra Studios, copper and blue glass sculpture. *Author's collection.*

Terra Studios, Fayetteville. *Author's collection.*

Paragould Meteorite

Folklore tells of a 1930 winter morning when two men driving a team of horses over a rural road entered an out-of-this-world experience. An enormous ball of fire with a long tail approached them from the northwest sky, illuminating the dark sky until night became day. The flaming ball passed over them at a tremendous speed, roaring like nothing they'd ever heard. Then came an unfathomable explosion, followed by a powerful shockwave that felt like an earthquake. They and the team of horses were knocked off their feet.

Historically, the men had experienced something of enormous consequence. The Paragould Meteorite fell to Earth at approximately 4:08 a.m. on February 17, 1930. Little could they have known the significance of the 820-pound meteorite, measuring sixteen inches by forty-one inches by twenty-four inches. They had witnessed the second-largest meteorite ever retrieved in North America and the largest stony meteorite ever found globally. The historic fireball was seen in Illinois, Indiana, Missouri and Kansas, and it caused an eight-foot crater at the crash site. The meteorite is now displayed at the Arkansas Center for Space and Planetary Sciences at the University of Arkansas–Fayetteville.

Tips for spotting Arkansas meteorites: look for them in the mountains rather than in deltas and valleys, where acidic soil and moving water can destroy them. Heavier than terrestrial rocks, meteorites are magnetic and have an irregular shape with smooth edges. Recent meteorites are black; older meteorites are weathered brown in color.

Chapter 14

TALES OF MOXIE, MYSTICISM AND HYSTERICAL STRENGTH

MARANDA JANE SIMMONS FRANCIS

Rumored to have lived for more than one hundred years, Maranda Jane Simmons beat the odds of life expectancy during her era. By the time Maranda smacked down Union soldiers during the American Civil War, she was middle aged at twenty-six. She expected to live about another twelve years, eighteen if she was lucky, but nobody could have predicted she'd be kicking for another seventy-eight years.

Maranda Jane oozed moxie vibes like a smashup blend of Granny Clampett and Gloria Steinem but without glasses—or teeth in later years. With life expectancy at thirty-eight years in her era, Maranda would come to question why in tarnation did the Almighty dole her more than one hundred revolutions around the sun. Family folklore claims she was too stubborn to die; longevity and a singing voice compose her legacy, along with a Civil War adventure that underscores an Ozark hillbilly woman's will to survive.

By family arrangement, she married John Francis in 1853, a man twenty years her senior. Maranda and John lived in the log cabin he built on farmland purchased through land grants for $1.25 per acre. Among rolling hills of Ozark country, the small one-room cabin with a dirt floor stood witness to earthquakes, tornadoes and cycles of drought that cracked the earth, as well as storms when the creek did rise.

The Civil War brought about division among the people of the state. No matter their sympathies, the reality of advancing troops into the Ozarks demanded that locals defend their land, animals and provisions necessary to survive the approaching winter. Thomas Jefferson described pro- and anti-slavery furor as a "fireball in the night."

John Francis had gone off to fight against the Union forces, as many civilians and soldiers alike joined to drive off the invading army that would confiscate their food and horses. It was not uncommon to find two or three generations of the same family fighting in the trenches in order to protect provisions they needed to survive the approaching winter months. With John gone, Maranda was left alone with three young children in October 1861 when Union troops camped on her farm. They murdered her brother, Gideon, who had stopped at the creek for water. A Union soldier shot him in the back.

John was absent from the homestead when Union soldiers apprehended their horses. When Maranda discovered they were missing, she assumed they had been taken to the Union camp. What she didn't know was whether John was alive. Acting as a widow dependent on those horses for survival, she lifted the shotgun from above the hand-crafted mantel and set out to reclaim her horses. With one baby on her hip and two others clinging to her skirt, she held tight to the shotgun in her right hand and marched right into the Union camp.

A freak Ozark thunderstorm didn't hinder her resolve; in fact, it may have helped. She likely resembled a mythical Ozark haint, visible only in flashes of lightning, appearing wild and crazy as swirling gusts of wind whipped her hair and clothes this way and that. For all the soldiers knew, she had used witchcraft to conjure the storm that blew into camp when her arrival instantly dropped the temperature by twenty degrees.

Maranda made such a ruckus as to gain the attention of the Union captain and demand he return her horses. He submitted to her request and ordered an escort back to her cabin—for her safety, as the story goes. One can only wonder if Union soldiers acted out of courtesy or fear.

Granny Clampett would have resonated with Maranda's adventure that night and would have taken Gloria Steinem to task, what with how the '60s feminist icon dismissed the traditional power of pioneer spirits as limited by a pre-suffragette world. Maranda, in her fury, personified Thomas Jefferson's label "fireball in the night" when the hillbilly woman smacked down Union forces without trepidation.

MINNIE BELL FRANCIS

Minnie Bell Francis (1895–1918). *Author's vintage photograph.*

The feather death crown, sometimes called an angel crown, is a swirl of feathers that forms in a feather pillow when someone dies. According to folklore, the crown is created precisely as the soul leaves the body, indicating the deceased was a good person and went directly to heaven. More information on the phenomenon can be found in chapter 9, where its folklore and origins are explained.

The mystery of the crown of Minnie Bell Francis was amplified when closer examination revealed a curious wool strand of teal-colored yarn descending from the underside. Small feathers pierced the twisted yarn strand at half-inch intervals, by design. It was a rare handcrafted fetish, a traditional witch's ladder, the heart and soul to rituals intended to heal or cast spells.

If raised hackles are proof of truth told, then this discovery confirmed the hushed secret that Bell had been a witch. Perhaps she, a farmer's daughter, was a healer gifted in the art of herbal remedies.

This is Bell's story, as told by the late George Knott, Francis family historian.

Minnie Bell Francis Irwin (1895–1918) was born and died in Ozark country. She inherited the Francis dark hair and brown eyes underscored by dark circles—the look of a mystic. She was the daughter of a farm couple, James Robert "Bob" Francis and Frances Louise "Fannie" Kennedy.

Married in 1911 at age sixteen, Bell had four children by age twenty-three. She met death in 1918, sometime after giving birth in January 1918 to twin girls in Nimmons, Arkansas. Baby Goldie died at age six months of anemia. Baby Daisy met death at age two during a measles epidemic.

Bell was a caulbearer and labeled a witch, an allegation supported by her feather death crown and its witch's ladder embedded in the core. Bell's daughter, granddaughter and great-granddaughter would wear the same label.

Bell's death certificate cannot be located and is presumed to have burned in the Clay County, Arkansas courthouse fire of 1921. However, the flu epidemic of 1918 may account for her demise. Bell's grave in Nimmons, Arkansas, washed away in the great flood of 1993.

GRACE MILDRED SOLLIS

Grace Sollis (1905–1992) was born and raised—or borned and raised, as she would say—in Arkansas. She was a small woman less than five feet tall, with blond hair and all-knowing greenish-brown eyes, plus a spunky streak that accompanied her well into her eighties. She could have stared down the Ozark Howler, if needed.

Hardship was a way of life during her childhood. After Grace lost her mother at a young age, her formal education ended at third grade. Her legacy is her creativity, intelligence and love of children and animals and the gardens she planted every year. She wrote poetry in folk art style and quoted scripture (especially prophecies) like a Pentecostal preacher at a tent revival. Grace Sollis Carroll is a woman about whom songs are written.

Her story, an oral family tradition, involves the phenomenon of superhuman strength in a crisis. It happened in Arkansas when she was a young mother living in a small cabin that was heated by a cast-iron wood-burning stove—a stove with a broken leg. An object was wedged under the bottom of the stove to keep it balanced and standing. Otherwise, it would fall.

Grace's story involves the day her small baby was crawling on the floor when his cotton gown caught and dislodged the object that was holding up the stove. It wobbled and then fell on top of the baby. Petite Grace picked up and moved that cast-iron stove in order to free her baby. She picked up the baby and ran straight out the front door, then ran circles around the house, holding the child to her breast until she came to her senses. The baby was unharmed, and Grace thanked God for a miracle.

She wrote the following collection of poems, which had lived in her mind's eye for decades. They are written in her hand on pages torn out of a personal phone book and on tablet paper now yellow and brittle with age. There is no punctuation, no periods or commas, no beginning and no end—an unintended metaphor of life and true example of folk poetry.

A Little Boy of Five
i wish I had a little dog to run and jump and play
i wish I had a kitty that would hide and play
i wish I could find my ball the nicest one I own
i wish I wouldn't wish so much
i wish mommy and daddy would come home

Green Frog
a little green frog sat next to a log
another little frog hopped on the log
and said let us go sailing today
so they hopped on a leaf
and the sun shone bright and the wind blew smooth
as they went sailing around the pool
and when they was tired and wanted to sleep
they hopped in the water and under a leaf
for they slept very tight for the rest of the night
and the little boat went sailing away

Untitled
i have went up hills an valee so low
i had my hart akes an truely been bless to
i have ben so weak I could hardly stand but god has tuek me by the hand
an for me open doors where life was pleason once more

#22 ARS Flood Water
it is raining to day so dark damp an cold
rivers and streams carrying the waters from montins an hills to vallies below
it is tragic and petifull to see with all the damage it has done
the water is muddie an is not pretty to see
washing down trees an goin down streets takin some homes an some lives
leaving the earth bear an clean bear
o god only noes why all this has happens
maby because we don't think an pray

#20 Snow
snow is pretty white
an the clouds above all white an clean makes the warter a butifull sen
an on the seders an pine an when the sun shin a shimer glow
But there some have lost there lives in this butifull snow so cold and white
so smothely lade over the hills an vallies the same

Mark
i seen a boy of 4 sittn in the yard playing in the dirt
close all dirty
his hair was red
frickels face
eyes black like crow
he was very besay at peas
jay bird set on a branch above
catcherin an calden at him above
for he had a nest with 4 babys he was garden keepin from harm
now the boy was bizzy with his toyes an didin seam to no that the birds
was up set

"Mark" poem by Grace Sollis Carroll, written on a page torn out of an address book, circa 1985. *Author's collection.*

Untitled
once I had kittie as white as the snow
she play in the barn a long time ago
had two little black eyes black as crow
an they spide little mouse a long time ago
a pear of teath had little kittl all in a row
an when they bit little mouse
little mousi crid ow
but little mouse got a way from kittie a long time ago

Pray for Me
When the sun is settin in
the golden west
an your mind clear an free
an you are prayin for others
Wood you some time pray for me

The lyrics that follow are from a song written about Grace Sollis Carroll by James Carroll, her grandson.

Seeds of Love
She lived her younger days close to the land
She carried her load twice as well as any man
The times they were rough, though they had little enough
Still she sowed the seeds of love along the path

She worked the day through while raising her young ones alone
Others as well from her learned the meaning of home
She's not of noble birth, but there's none of greater worth
She sowed the seeds of love along the path

She's seen many smiles and she's cried many tears
As she blessed the young ones and parted with others so dear
With heartache she's no stranger, but it never could restrain her
As she sowed the seeds of love along the path

She loves her garden, she'd grow one every year
She'd work the ground and tend it with great care

116

And as she'd watch it grow, I'd wonder does she know
How she's sown the seeds of love along the path
She'll say live a good life, enjoy what God has made
She'd sing us a rhyme and as children we'd laugh and play
And now that we're grown, we're better for having known
The one who's sown the seeds of love along the path

Chapter 15

OZARK ANOMALIES NORTH OF THE ARKANSAS BORDER

JOPLIN SPOOK LIGHTS

The Joplin Lights appear in an area known locally as the Devil's Promenade on the border between southwestern Missouri and northeastern Oklahoma, west of Hornet, Missouri. The lights are visible from the Missouri towns of Joplin and Hornet and the Oklahoma border near the town of Quapaw. Like the sun and moon, the lights travel east to west.

To get to a good viewing spot, take I-44 to exit 4 (Highway 86 South), then drive six miles to junction Route BB. Turn right on BB Highway and follow the road until it ends. Turn right again, go one mile and then turn left on E50 Road (also known as Spooklight Road). About two miles into the road is the darkest and best place to wait for the lights to appear.

The Joplin Lights have been reported since the early nineteenth century. First encounters date back to the Trail of Tears in the 1830s. Sightings are documented from 1881, with the earliest published report from the *Kansas City Star* circa 1936. The lights became more well known after World War II, and by the 1960s the road would frequently be jammed with vehicles loaded with sightseers hoping to see them. According to locals, the best time to view the Joplin Lights is between the hours of 10:00 p.m. and midnight. The lights reportedly avoid large groups and loud sounds.

The Joplin Lights have been termed "mysterious lights of unknown origin" by the U.S. Army Corps of Engineers. Other studies define them as distant highway lights on the Oklahoma side. In early sightings, they were reported as floating in the forest or over open land. In other reports, the glowing orbs appear on the path, swinging side to side or rolling on the ground but always staying on the path. Some describe the lights as dancing and spinning at high speeds down the center of the road. They rise above treetops and then hover before retreating and vanishing. They have appeared nightly for over one hundred years.

Though many paranormal and scientific investigators have studied the lights, including members of the Army Corps of Engineers, no one has been able to provide a conclusive answer as to what they are or where they originate. Explanations are lame at best, such as blaming escaping natural gas, common in marshy areas, that self-ignites. The Joplin Lights are not in a marshy area, so there is no gas and no self-igniting.

The notion that the lights are reflections or car lights is easily debunked because they appeared before the advent of automobiles and before roads existed in the area. Some suggest the lights are caused by will-o'-the-wisp, a luminescence created by rotting organic matter, but will-o'-the-wisp lacks the intense luminosity of the Joplin Lights. One possible explanation that is not as easily discounted regards the Joplin Lights as an electrical atmospheric charge. This area is on a fault line running east to west from New Madrid, Missouri, where shifting rocks deep below the earth's surface create pressure that can result in seismoluminescence, or electrical charge resulting from pressure.

Numerous legends exist to describe the origin of the lights. The oldest lore is about a Quapaw Indian maiden who fell in love with a young brave. When her father would not allow them to marry, they eloped. Pursued by a party of warriors, the couple joined hands above Spring River and jumped to their deaths.

Another tells of a miner whose cabin was attacked by Indians while he was away, and his wife and children went missing. Legend says he continues to look for them along the old road, using a lantern to light the path.

Some believe the lights are the ghost of an Osage Indian chief searching for his decapitated head, using a lantern to light the path. Frankly, this is too cliché to believe, and why would a decapitated head need a lantern to light the path anyway? I mean, really.

The Joplin Lights are located at the crossroads of three states: Missouri, Oklahoma and Kansas. For unknown reasons, crossroad energy tends to attract paranormal activity. Perhaps this tri-state crossroads energy and its association with the Trail of Tears has validity.

Not only are the Joplin Lights a mystical paradox, but in addition, a paranormal element permeates the crossroads. A major tectonic fault line runs through the area: the New Madrid (Missouri) fault line. The worst earthquakes in recorded history occurred along the New Madrid fault line in 1812, causing the Mississippi River to run backward for a time. Tectonic plates along a fault line create intense pressure in the underlying rock and can cause an electric charge to be expressed from the ground rather than the sky. Many believe that ley lines run the path of tectonic faults. I'm just sayin'.

THE RUNAWAY MOUNTAIN COASTER

The Runaway Mountain Coaster uses the natural mountain topography of the Ozarks to power a roller coaster down the mountain. Like a traditional roller coaster, riders are settled in individual carts that are pulled to the highest point by a chain. At the top of the mountain, carts are released to freefall down the mountainside on a track, winding in and out of the forest and around trees for the thrill of a lifetime.

This mountain coaster is specially designed to preserve the natural beauty of the woodland setting and offers the choice of either a slower trip down the track or the fastest and most exciting ride possible. The speed is determined by a hand brake the rider controls.

The Runaway Mountain Coaster is located just over the northern Arkansas border near Branson, Missouri.

MISSOURI GRAND CANYON

Deep in the paranormal highway territory, Missouri's Grand Gulf State Park, also known as the Little Grand Canyon, is the remnant of an ancient collapsed dolomite cave system. Dolomite is a sedimentary rock composed of the mineral dolomite. Found in sedimentary basins worldwide, dolomite forms from lime mud and limestone reacting to magnesium-rich groundwater. Designated as one of the natural wonders of the Ozarks, Grand Gulf State Park presents the most spectacular Ozark collapsed cave system. It is a geologic preserve operated by the State of Missouri on privately owned land accessible to the public. It's located on Highway W in Thayer, Missouri.

Thayer is a rural railroad town named after the railroad promoter Nathaniel Thayer, and it was laid out in 1882 as a railway.

Grand Gulf State Park is an example of karst topography and underground stream piracy. Karst topography forms when soluble rocks such as limestone, dolomite and gypsum dissolve, creating caves and underground drainage systems. Stream piracy is defined as a geomorphological phenomenon that occurs when a stream or river drainage system or watershed is diverted from its own bed and flows instead into the bed of an adjoining stream. These twenty-eight square miles of watershed drain into a cave entrance on the eastern end and emerge about nine miles away in Mammoth Spring, Arkansas.

The Grand Gulf State Park stretches more than a mile between 130-foot-high sheer bluffs. Its 322 acres include one of the largest natural bridges in Missouri, which is the remaining section of the cave ceiling and spans 250 feet. Visitors can walk under the 75-foot-high natural bridge on the canyon floor, or they can see it from trails around the rim.

Here we find another setting involving paranormal alchemy, railroad tracks, quartz limestone and moving water—set in the paranormal highway where UFOs are frequently seen in these rural Missouri skies.

HAINTS AND HOLLOWS ROAD TRIP

Mystery and folklore are born wherever moving water, quartz crystal and iron exist collectively. By the same token, you'll find these elements at the core of any good ghost story. My St. Louis childhood in historic neighborhoods at the banks of the Mississippi River has them all in abundance. Historic Soulard and its sister neighborhood Benton Park were built using limestone block imbedded with quartz crystal and iron-rich red clay brick. Cherokee Cave and English Cave, formed by eons of Mississippi River currents, exist beneath these historic neighborhoods.

Living in a haunted row house above this epicenter of paranormal alchemy during a gypsy-style childhood is what instigated us Irish twin sisters, later in life, to scheme an off-the-beaten-path road trip through the Arkansas Ozarks that ended with spending Halloween night in a haunted hotel on a dare—the most haunted hotel in the country.

Come along with me and my Irish twin, Sheree, by way of the printed page, and I'll show how it happened.

"Sheree, we'll be within striking distance of the most haunted hotel in the country. On Halloween," I touted. I really piled it high and deep with animated body language and verbal inflection. My sister, no doubt, realized I'd just ballyhooed a dare.

"That's what I'm talking about, Cyn," she said and nodded to signal she accepted the challenge. Wearing a devilish grin, she dialed the 1886 Crescent Hotel and reserved a room. The prepaid reservation included two ghost tour tickets. The room charge was no chump change—no turning back.

We had two travel days to arrive there on Halloween, too many shenanigans and so little time. From Houston, Texas, to Eureka Springs, Arkansas, without the bother of Rand McNally or interstate highways and with copies of *A Ghost in My Suitcase* and *Off the Beaten Path Arkansas* riding shotgun on the console—well, what could go wrong with Irish twins and unbridled sibling rivalry.

We are daughters of generations of mystics. Resident ghosts and levitating Uncle Patrick at Grandmother's house for entertainment on Sunday afternoon was normal fanfare during our childhood among cobblestone streets during the Atomic Age. Our Benton Park playground was once a makeshift city cemetery put up in the 1840s during a yellow fever epidemic. Really.

Our lifelong rivalry brewed up an eventful road trip through the Arkansas Ozark Mountains, where water moves through rock to form natural springs, where the iron-rich red soil is home to crystal mines. The trinity of paranormal elements was inherent all along the path.

First off, we'd hit some east Texas hot spots traveling the Lone Star State between my Houston home and northwestern Arkansas. The Big Thicket, Saratoga's Bragg Road ghost lights and Jefferson—the most haunted town in Texas—headlined the Texas itinerary.

I use the word "itinerary" as a loosey-goosey point of reference because I believe the journey *is* the destination and unforeseen encounters that happen out of the blue are often more memorable than what's planned.

BIG THICKET NATIONAL RESERVE, TEXAS

A nature reserve is a protected area of importance for flora, fauna or features of geological or other special interest that is reserved and managed for conservation and research. Such is the Big Thicket National Reserve of Texas, which is not only of interest for flora and fauna but is also known for UFO and Sasquatch sightings and for the Bragg Road ghost lights of Saratoga.

I first heard about the Bragg Road ghost lights from someone who experienced them firsthand. Brenda, an eccentric Texas writer, divulged the following stranger-than-fiction tale that left me wondering if she was a natural-born flake.

She began the Bragg Road mystery lights saga with a story about the time she bought a hand grenade at a neighborhood garage sale. Later that night, it occurred to Brenda that the explosive device might be, well, dangerous. The risk factor made her jumpy, so she put the grenade in the trunk of her car and drove it to the police station at about two o'clock in the morning. When she walked into the station holding a grenade, the ensuing chain of events included an emergency precinct evacuation just before the bomb squad arrived.

Brenda's lucky break with a grenade upstages her Big Thicket mystery lights exploit, even though blue orbs landed on her grandchildren and she has photos to prove it.

Today, my red Xterra's five on the floor offered the means for my sister's edgy reunion with the art of driving a stick shift. She aced easy breezy east Texas on flat state Highway 59 right up to Saratoga's Bragg Road, located in the exact middle of nowhere. She hadn't worked a manual transmission in, oh, say, thirty years, not since our shared cobalt blue VW bug in high school during the late '60s when we were cool. In hindsight, I should have prepared her for the Bragg Road ghost lights, as well as UFO and Sasquatch sightings. But no.

Bragg Road, named for Confederate general Braxton Bragg, is eight miles of red gravel road, the former location of a Santa Fe Railroad line. Swamp water flanks each side of the narrow lane where oil, logs and cattle were transported by rail until the tracks were removed in 1934 and the lights began to appear. The rails are long gone, but the mystery lives on.

Mystery lights appear at random but are best seen in the thicket's pitch-black loblolly pine forest. They shy away during the full moon, obviously intimidated by dancing moon shadows in the biodiverse swamp. I can't say I blame them. Sasquatch sightings support the notion of a Bigfoot parallel universe where they slip in and out of sight. UFO sightings are more common than fireflies.

Bragg Road folklore keeps alive its version of the ubiquitous headless conductor swinging a lantern while searching for his decapitated head. Another tradition has a missing hunter trying to find his way home. Yet another has a newlywed husband searching for his murdered bride. Some believe the lights are lost souls from a Mexican cemetery, spirits of men who were murdered by a roadcrew foreman who preferred killing them to paying wages. The fallback explanation for the mystery lights is to say swamp gas is the culprit—the theory of skeptics.

It's anybody's guess if my pink canister of pepper spray paired with a trumped-up AAA membership kept us incognito at Bragg Road, but not one Saratoga ghost light appeared, nor did a UFO abduct anybody. Sadly, we had no annoying Sasquatch encounter, nor did we slip into the thicket's legendary parallel universe. So far as we know.

After leaving Bragg Road like bats out of hell in the moonlight, we headed northbound on Highway 59 toward our next destination: Jefferson, Texas.

JEFFERSON, TEXAS

Although Jefferson is noted as the most haunted town in the Lone Star State, and although many famous people have stayed here over the years, the most talked about haunt involves the night during the early 1970s when Steven Spielberg checked into the Excelsior Hotel. He and a film crew were scouting the area for a location to film a movie. Spielberg checked into the J Gould room, known to have the most paranormal activity. Whether this was intentional or a coincidence will remain unknown. Late in the night, he awoke to find a little boy sitting on his bed and asking him if he was ready for breakfast. Spielberg and his crew packed up and left town at about two o'clock in the morning. This was pre-*Poltergeist*, y'all!

I first heard about Jefferson when a clever book titled *A Ghost in My Suitcase* caught my eye at Barnes and Noble. It seems the book chose me rather than the other way around. From a display table, it beckoned, "Hey you, over here, buy me." And so, I did.

Named for President Thomas Jefferson, this charming tourist destination in east Texas knows how to reinvent itself. It was once a river port, and trade with Louisiana sustained Jefferson until a natural log dam, known as Red River Raft, broke apart in 1873 and the river all but dried up. It left the once prosperous river port sitting in the middle of nowhere, like an oasis. Currently, its quaint downtown and estate mansions, now bed-and-breakfast destinations, give rise to tourist interest for paranormal conferences and weekly ghost tours.

A Ghost in My Suitcase, by local writer Mitchel Whitington, initiated my interest in Jefferson, now one of my favorite places to visit. Whitington lives in this town, in what is noted as the most haunted house in the most haunted Texas town, and he offers tours of his circa 1861 home known as The Grove.

The day my sister and I toured The Grove marks Sheree's attempt to parallel park the Xterra. In front of Whitington's residence on sleepy Moseley Street, her effort is worthy of headlining the local paper, the *Jefferson Jimplecute*. The Xterra was the only car in sight on the muddy street, but little did we know the parking spectacle foreshadowed what would unfold the following day when she navigated mountain terrain driving the standard transmission five on the floor.

The Grove stands as a regional example of Jefferson's ties to riverboat trade with Louisiana during the 1800s. The one-story residential building blends two architectural styles, Greek Revival and French Creole. Its symmetrical Greek Revival exterior fronts an asymmetrical French Creole interior that is supported by ancient Louisiana cypress beams. French Creole style mandates each room open directly into the next, without the bother of hallways. Perhaps changes to The Grove that have happened over time confuse the melting pot of spirits that haunt it, with both intelligent and residual hauntings.

A residual haunting is when a ghost repeats the same action over and over, like a movie on perpetual replay. There is no interaction of the ghost with the living. Such is the full-body apparition of a woman wearing a long white dress who walks into the house through an exterior side wall. In the history of The Grove, a door was located on that side of the property, where a porch stood before changes were made. Additionally, former residents often pass through the house as residual haunts.

An intelligent haunting involves a ghost who interacts with the living. Such is the male spirit guardian who sometimes confronts curiosity seekers with a vintage shotgun. Likewise, phantom Basset hounds that were pets of the Whitingtons' return for occasional visits.

Mitchel Whitington and his wife, Tammy, project a positive vibe about The Grove and believe that for reasons unknown, the land is accessible for spirits to pass through the veil that separates our worlds. Not only do the Whitingtons love living in The Grove, but they believe they were chosen to be its caretakers. Whitington mentions that he has been mistaken as a ghostly figure haunting the front porch, relaxing in a rocking chair and drinking his favorite coffee, and someday he hopes to enjoy that destiny. What with his mane of long white hair, either scenario seems plausible.

Smitten with charming Jefferson's specters and flesh-and-blood cast of players, we sisters found it difficult to say goodbye to the retro general store and five-cent cups of coffee. Au revoir to Creole architecture, adios ghost train and swamp tours and farewell all y'all stacked cornbread ham sandwiches and Creole gumbo.

ARKANSAS, THE NATURAL STATE

After another two hours northbound on Highway 59, we sisters rolled into the Natural State, suspended in darkness, by way of Texarkana beneath a black velvet sky and canopy of never-ending stars.

The Arkansas state name is derived from the Quapaw Indians who once populated the land. Other early residents were of Scotch-Irish descent, so my Irish twin and I blended with little effort. The Natural State has a unique essence that melds the wild frontier spirit with the well-mannered spirit of the Old South.

Few states can claim geography that includes such varied features as the flat Mississippi Delta alongside rugged peaks and gorges of the Ozark and Quachita Mountains. These mountains are one of only a few ranges globally that have an east–west orientation. They offer panoramic woodland views and showcase lush forests of hardwoods and pines among 500,000 acres of lakes and ancient springs.

HOT SPRINGS

Arriving in Arkansas beneath a silver crescent moon over the horizon, the stretch to Hot Springs was easygoing, right up until getting lost in the sportsman's wilderness and fearing we'd succumb to huntin' and fishin' a survivor's path to Holiday Inn. I'm not claiming alien abduction; yet I can't rule it out, what with unaccounted whereabouts and a substantial chunk of missing time. Sometime after midnight, we finally collapsed into hotel beds, the morning sun nipping at our heels and anxious to reveal Ozark rolling hills marked by fire colors.

After exploring Hot Springs for all things weird, we sisters concluded freaky Bath House Row topped the list. We left Hot Springs feeling all hoity-toity driving toward the Quachita Mountains, but something strange happened at the outskirts of town when the Xterra nudged toward the tourist center, where a public water feature dispensed hot spring water free for the taking. The fountain features about a dozen spigots that dispense natural spring water that has traveled underground for four thousand years before it breaks the surface at 145 degrees Fahrenheit.

The stop for magical spring water went south when Sheree's spigot malfunctioned. Rather than filling the gallon container she held, water shot up ten feet into the air and then arced back down when gravity took hold, drenching my sister head to toe, respectively. Without mercy, a hootenanny dance claimed her. Had six generations of our Ozark ancestral DNA surfaced with that spring water? The secret life of ancient springs presented its frank sense of humor to this pair of Pisces Irish twins, one now baptized by water meeting the light of day after four thousand years in darkness. I stood there, jaw-dropping astounded and wide-eyed, watching it happen in slow motion.

JESSIEVILLE

Sheree was in rocket mode when she put the pedal to the metal and launched the Xterra north on Arkansas Highway 7. Hot Springs receded into the distance, its historic buildings replaced by mile after mile of sinuous curved road meandering through sloping Ozark landscape and valley streams among the most beautiful canopy of fall color in recent history.

All through Texas and Arkansas, Sheree scored a passing grade on handling a five-speed transmission, but she blew it negotiating the Quachitas. The Xterra dragged and gyrated along uphill drudges, while a snarky transmission seemed to say *love me tender and call me Elvis.*

"What should I do?" she asked frantically.

"Just feel it, Sheree. Be the transmission. Elvis will tell you when to shift," I said, all Zen-like on the road flanked by runaway truck ramps, unaware that a runaway ramp is how you stop a forty-ton missile from taking out everything in its path.

"Really, Buddha? If that's true, why didn't you *be* the spigot back at the springs?" she asked.

Excellent point, but had I been the spigot, the outcome would have been the same. I kept that thought to myself. No need to stir that pot.

Driving through an area referred to as Lost Atlantis had a mysterious impact on my sister. Perhaps the water that once covered Lost Atlantis surfaced thousands of years later in the geyser that drenched my sister and set her off. Perhaps those limestone hills loaded with quartz crystal generated enough paranormal energy to mess with her chakras. It's anyone's guess, but what I can say for sure is this: she got weirder by the minute near a crystal dig site along the isolated Arkansas rural highway, depending on what appeared in the rearview mirror.

Although we rarely saw another car, she'd freak out if one showed up in the mirror. Trancelike, she'd drift over the center rumble strip and set off a riveting wake-up call to all living creatures, foreign and domestic.

"Oh my God, I can't help it. I get nervous when I see another car," she said.

Once again, elements that support paranormal activity were present: moving water, quartz crystal and iron. A palpable atmospheric transformation occurred as we approached the thirty-seventh parallel between the Boston Mountains and Fayetteville. The parallel band is known as the paranormal highway, where UFO sightings underscore theories of aliens among us who live unseen in the intricate network of subterranean caves.

EUREKA SPRINGS

Aliens at the thirty-seventh parallel and ghosts aside, there is no disputing that Eureka Springs is a source of paranormal activity or that it has been an area of curiosity since ancient times. The Victorian resort town listed in the National Register of Historic Places attracts artists and writers, musicians and naturalists. Quirky people from all walks populate the town, as well as Eureka Springs Cemetery located on Magnetic Mountain.

Eureka Springs, northeast of the Boston Mountains, encounters a phenomenon known as a sky quake, or thunder during a clear sky. Having experienced the phenomenon personally, I can say that humans react to a sky quake much like the tornado-predicting hogs of weather folklore.

Having avoided the legendary Ozark Howler thus far, we courageously pressed on. The bear-sized mythical creature with shaggy black hair and horns lives in remote areas of Arkansas. The Howler's telltale cry is described as the melding of a wolf's howl and elk's bugle. Thankfully, rumble strip thunder hadn't disturbed the Ozark Howler, which might have mistaken it as a bellowing mating call.

I was at the wheel when we rolled into Eureka Springs later that evening among Halloween shadows that mimicked shapeshifting otherworldly creatures in pale moonlight.

"Turn here!" navigator Sheree commanded alongside a steep turnoff.

This required a severe left turn that curved back on itself and disappeared into a wooded incline as steep as they come. One side was a soaring limestone bluff, the other an abyss.

I involuntarily held my breath while downshifting to first gear and gunning the engine for a forty-five-degree running start. Cog by cog, Elvis ascended the limestone angle with the clutch pad smoking like a bad omen. I feared the reach had exceeded the grasp on this one, feared rolling backward and waking up dead in a ditch.

My life didn't flash before me, but I did ask myself this question: How did I get to this moment in my life, moving through space and time on the paranormal highway, suspended in darkness atop a limestone mountain and driving a smoking SUV named Elvis? Adding fuel to the fire, I am headed toward a haunted hotel and ghost tour, all the while keeping an ear to the ground in case of the hormone-infused Ozark Howler or wood-carrying hogs or thunderous sky quakes. On Halloween.

As we crested the peak, an eight-foot-tall doppelgänger of Glinda the Good Witch came into focus on a residential building. Not only that, the garage roof was constructed in the shape of a pointed witch's hat.

"Are you a good witch or a bad witch?" I asked Sheree, even though I knew the answer.

THE 1886 CRESCENT HOTEL

The 1886 Crescent Hotel and Spa sits atop the limestone crescent-shaped mountain like a paranormal beacon. We arrived just in the nick of time to catch the ghost tour, which attracted about sixty people, paranormal enthusiasts and skeptics alike, couples and families and the surprisingly skittish Harley crowd passing through on an annual foliage ride. People oozed through narrow hotel hallways and staircases during the two-hour tour, like slow-moving bayou sludge.

Featured was the building's history that began when Irish stonemasons arrived in 1884 to construct the eighteen-inch-thick limestone walls. A stonemason named Michael fell to his death during construction and haunts room 218, the hotel's most requested room. The Crescent College and Conservatory for Young Women occupied the building from 1908 to 1934. One young student fell from a balcony and is said to haunt the hotel. The question remains: did she jump, or was she pushed? By 1937, the charlatan Norman Baker had turned the building into Baker's Cancer-Curing Hospital, where many patients arrived, many died and many remain to haunt the building.

Tour guide Carroll Heath chose me out of the crowd to assist him in demonstrating the energy field that exists around all people. He asked me to face him and hold my hands up next to his, with fingers pointed toward the ceiling.

"Without touching me, what do you feel?" he asked.

"My fingers are tingling, and I feel lightheaded," I said, wondering if ghosts were present or if Carroll's psychic power carried a punch. Perhaps I stood in an energy vortex. A photograph shows us two Carrolls standing with a blue orb floating above our fingertips.

"That's good," he said. "Blue signifies communication."

Seventy-eight-year-old Carroll Heath concluded the tour sitting on a vintage autopsy table in what had served as the basement morgue during the building's tenure as a hospital. About then, a few tourists found it difficult to breathe. They fled, and then others followed like a colony of bats leaving Carlsbad Cavern at sunset. First one, then in pairs and then en masse. Some stayed to hear gruesome tales of preserved body parts and tumors housed in mason jars that once lined the morgue storage shelves like pickled produce. What a perfect Halloween in a haunted hotel that earned the designation as the holy grail of paranormal activity during filming of *Ghost Hunters*!

After the tour, Sheree and I wandered haunted hallways and snapped hundreds of photographs that captured swarms of orbs and rods of bizarre lights. Passion's rhythm amplified by squeaky bed springs rang through the haunted hotel halls like the Bells of Rhymney.

"Be the springs, Sheree," I touted.

Exhausted once again, we sisters settled into our room, far too scared to turn out the lights. What with the smell of pipe tobacco hinting at the infamous Norman Baker, plus a poke in the behind by a notorious little boy haunt, anybody would have been jumpy.

"Something just poked my be-hind," I said, whirling around to accuse my sister.

"Well, don't look at me!" she said from across the room, harboring insult.

"I'm not kidding. I thought it was you, until I turned around and saw you all the way over there," I said. With fifteen feet between us, she couldn't have done it. Cool.

Sheree manically sprinted into the bathroom in epiphany mode, collected bath towels and returned to cover the dresser mirror.

"What the heck are you doing?" I asked.

"Covering the mirror traps spirits in there for the night," she said, astounded that I didn't know about such a basic tactic.

"Well, you know they are your towels, right?" I smirked.

Sheree gained rivalry points by taking the bed nearest the dresser and its haunted mirror. But she lost some by being closest to the room's only exit. With my bed located farthest from the exit, I was chicken shit to my core but didn't show weakness by crawling into bed with my sister that spooky night. I'd have scared her to death and one-upped our rivalry, but I don't want payback on that grand scale.

I tuned the television to a Billy Joel documentary that looped all night. The piano man sang us to twilight sleep while every light in the room blazed on Halloween on a limestone mountain. Thank you, Billy Joel.

There's no telling what went on in there after we went to sleep.

GLOSSARY OF PARANORMAL TERMS

ESP: Extra Sensory Perception, or ESP, is a term that describes the ability of some people to perceive things beyond their five senses of sight, sound, touch, smell and taste. Also known as second sight or sixth sense, ESP doesn't function like, nor is it dependent on, any of our five senses. Age, location, time or intelligence has no bearing. Some believe ESP originates from another reality to bring information to people about the past, present or future. A person with the power of ESP is known as psychic.

The most popular theory for the phenomenon of ESP is that it is a primitive sense everyone experiences, but with the advancement of society where we rely less on our intuition, we have become less aware. Most people believe that they have had at least one ESP experience in their life. Animals, particularly dogs, cats and horses, have been known to display it. Time and again, people will recount odd behavior in animals just before a natural disaster or impending danger.

Clairvoyance is the ability to see beyond the normal realm of sight. Clairsentience is psychic knowledge gained through touch. Clairaudience is the ability to hear beyond the realm of normal. Clairalience is psychic information gained by smell. Clairgustance is the ability to taste a substance.

Under the banner of clairvoyance, one sees people, places, objects or events set in the past, present or future. Mirrors and crystal balls, along with visions and dreams, are often vehicles for clairvoyance. Spirits in the form of ghosts, mists, fairies, sprites or shadow people appear to some people. A clairsentience experience includes reading an object by touch, such as an antique piece of jewelry. Also known as psychometry, touching a person or object will reveal information. With clairaudience, one hears a voice or laughter; with clairalience, one smells tobacco, perfume or flowers significant to a person or event; and with clairgustance, one tastes a substance significant to a person or event.

hysterical strength: Hysterical strength is a display of extreme strength by humans beyond what is believed to be possible, usually occurring when people are in life-and-death situations. Common anecdotal examples include parents lifting vehicles to rescue their children. Hysterical strength occurs during a crisis involving danger or fear. It is sometimes known as "fight or flight."

ley line: Ley lines are categorized as earth mysteries, a field of study into ancient sites and their surrounding landscapes. They are prehistoric alignments of earth energy and are found in patterns of powerful, invisible, straight lines of energy that run along and beneath the earth's surface. They connect sacred sites or other locations of spiritual or magical importance. Some paranormal enthusiasts believe that fissures in tectonic plates move magnetic energy along ley lines. The point where one ley line crosses another is a powerful source of paranormal energy.

Churches and their adjacent cemeteries, stone circles and megaliths are often found along ley lines, as are some cemeteries that are not on church ground. Some attribute the crop circle phenomenon as connected to the mystery lines. Ley lines are thought to possess spiritual, astrological and healing qualities.

The phrase *ley line* was first coined by Alfred Watkins, an English beer salesman, which might account for his ability to think out of the box. An amateur antiquarian researcher, the beer salesman noticed, in 1921, that ancient mounds, burial sites and churches were built in straight lines throughout the United Kingdom. He published a book titled *The Old Straight Track* in 1925. Watkins surmised the ley lines (meaning grassy tracks) were remnants of prehistoric trading paths, but the concept of ley lines and their locations soon grew to include a worldwide network. The mysterious earth energy might have been sensed by the early humans who used the prehistoric paths and by builders of the old churches. Some dowsers are successful in locating ley lines as the flow of universal life force, or chi, found in feng shui.

It is a stretch of the imagination to accept the concept of ley lines when you can't engage your five senses to experience them. How is a ley line detectable when it's invisible, silent, tasteless, scentless and untouchable? Is it possible to have experienced the power of a ley line without knowing what it was?

Consider what happened when Suzan Saxman, author of *The Reluctant Psychic*, visited Glastonbury. In her memoir, she talks about her attraction to the remains of an ancient church and gardens and sacred well. Without knowing its history, Saxman stood on the ground and felt energy rising out of the earth into the soles of her feet. It coursed through her body and then moved out of the crown of her head. She likens the experience to an awakening accompanied by the sensation of pure joy.

Adopting the notion that intersecting ley lines are points where paranormal phenomena, such as UFO sightings, earth lights and hauntings, occur is a springboard to exploring Arkansas and its intersecting ley lines. The notion of the earth mystery known as ley lines revealed itself to me personally two times, both in cemeteries. Many people adopt the belief that a grid of earth energies circles the globe, connecting the obvious sacred sites of antiquity, such as Stonehenge, the Egyptian pyramids and the Great Wall of China. Are my Texas and Arkansas locations as sacred as the Glastonbury locations from antiquity that Saxman came upon?

orb: The type of orb that is sometimes labeled as paranormal is a round circle of light that appears to float and drift in the air. The phenomenon is contemplated in paranormal circles, but there are methods to judge the authenticity of an orb as something paranormal. Orb enthusiasts are convinced the spheres are visible evidence of spirit energy, while others believe they are simply dust or humidity. Whatever orbs may be, they are seen globally, day or night, in all seasons, whether invited or not and whether you believe they are of paranormal significance or simply dust. Orbs can sometimes be seen by the naked eye. For the most part, they appear in photographs, especially photographs taken with a camera that engages a flash and especially when the flash has the feature to reduce the reflecting red in the eyes. Some theorize a camera's strobe flash positively charges the orb, a situation that causes it to show up in a photograph. Whether orbs are a paranormal phenomenon or dust particles, there's no doubt that most people have captured them on film at one time or another.

Orb characteristics: There is no way to prove the paranormal nature of an orb captured on film, but their color and intensity can indicate authenticity. A bright orb that is opaque is considered a very good find.

In the paranormal sense, the color of an orb relates to colors associated with energy. Warm (or fire) colors are red, yellow and orange. In the art world, an artist uses warm colors to indicate emotions or passion. Cool (or earth) colors are green and blue-green for a cool forest and blue for cool water. An artist uses warm colors to indicate calmness. Warm and cool colors translate to the paranormal realm as well. Here are some general examples.

White or clear orbs look more like a transparent circle with light reflected around its edges. They often appear in a location where something significant has happened, such as a Civil War battlefield. White or silver orbs indicate spirituality, a connection with a higher source. White energy is considered to be very positive and protective.

Warm colors: Red or orange orbs are associated with safety, security and belonging. Pink orbs signify messengers of love: universal love, the presence of a deceased loved one. They bring the message of encouragement, hope and peace. Warm colors are associated with emotions like anger or passion. Paranormal investigators believe a red or orange orb indicates a spirit who was a protector or caretaker in life.

Cool colors: Green orbs are associated with matters of the heart. Because they also represent nature, a green orb could indicate the presence of a human spirit rather than one who has never been in human form. Blue orbs signify spirits associated with psychic energy and truth and may signify a calming spirit.

Dark colors: Brown or black orbs indicate lower spiritual vibrations or heavy energy. The area in which they appear may contain negative energy or may be unsafe. A large brown orb appeared on one of my photographs taken near the morgue of the 1886 Crescent Hotel. Gray orbs may indicate spiritual depression or spiritual lack, fear, confusion or trouble.

The meaning of an orb's color can be interpreted more subjectively, such as what the color means to you personally or how you relate to the color. For example, if your childhood blankie was blue (a cool color) and your association to blue is warm and fuzzy, then go with that personal association.

Shape and intensity: Having considered the meaning of an orb based on its color, consider that its intensity has significance as well. Orbs, by definition, appear as circles. Orbs seen by the naked eye, in a photograph or on a video take on other characteristics. Orbs in photos appear two dimensional, round and flat. Many people believe they see faces inside the orb. Orbs in videos look three-dimensional, round with height, depth and width. Orbs seen with the naked eye look three-dimensional and emit their own source of light. Bright opaque orbs are the best find. Thinner transparent orbs are likely only dust.

The actual size of an orb may be an optical illusion. A small orb that is close will appear larger, but a large orb that is more distant will appear smaller.

Whether orbs are of a paranormal origin or they are dust or humidity or an optical illusion, just chill out and approach them with an attitude of curiosity. Save the fear and hysteria for fictional movies designed to frighten, and then have some fun exploring the upbeat paranormal with an open mind.

portal: According to *The Element Encyclopedia of the Psychic World*, the portal theory occurs at sites where there is an opening to another dimension where spirits can travel between the spirit and physical worlds. Sacred places around the world are thought to be gateways for spirits. Portals open at places where intense violence or trauma occurred, such as battlefields or hospitals, as well as lonely places like lighthouses or graveyards.

seismoluminescence or earthquake lights: Seismoluminescence is lights flashed from the ground, caused by quartz crystals under pressure. (Note: this is documented in the events that took place prior to the 1811–12 New Madrid, Missouri earthquakes. For an interesting read on strange things that happened during the series of quakes, see www.new-madrid.mo.us/132/Strange-Happenings-during-the-Earthquake.)

sky quake: This is an unexplained phenomenon that sounds like a cannon or a sonic boom coming from a clear sky.

types of hauntings: A haunting is defined as phenomena caused by ghosts and spirits. The phenomena manifest in apparitions, unusual changes in temperature, movement of objects, unusual smells and noises with no apparent source.

Ghosts are rarely seen, but the ones that are seen are reported as resembling real people. They can appear in solid form or may look transparent. Most hauntings involve noises such as sighs and whispers, smells such as perfume or burning wood, sensations such as raised hackles on the skin or cold breezes or being touched.

A *residual haunting* repeats the same action over and over, like a movie on perpetual replay. There is no interaction of the ghost with the living. Some believe residual hauntings are a form of psychometry, or vibrations of events and emotions imprinted into a building or object. A residual haunting is often a reenactment of historical events or a great tragedy. The ghost has no awareness of nor interaction with the living. It is defined as the result of psi energy imprinted on the environment and replayed time and again endlessly.

Psi is the twenty-third letter of the Greek alphabet, and its energy is associated with psychic or paranormal phenomena. Additionally, psi operates outside the boundaries of space and time, and it is not affected by the laws of physics, thermodynamics or gravity. It doesn't require exchange of energy, nor is it governed by the laws of relativity, which holds that nothing can move faster than the speed of light.

Some paranormal theorists claim that the presence of quartz crystal can be a component to a residual haunting in that the crystal behaves as an energy source that captured the original event and plays it over and over, like a memory.

An *intelligent haunting* involves a ghost that interacts with the living. Some hauntings result when the spirit of a person or animal is trapped on earth and doesn't know how to leave.

A *grateful dead* haunting involves a ghost that returns to repay a favor or kindness received in life.

A *poltergeist* is a mischievous ghost capable of making disturbances such as loud noises and moving objects around.

vortex: A vortex is defined as a spiral motion that draws in energy toward its center. In the natural world, tornadoes, dirt devils and hurricanes are types of vortexes. In the supernatural realm, a vortex or energy portal, such as those that exist in Sedona, Arizona, is invisible to the eye but felt by the body. Raised hackles, dizziness, nausea or butterflies in the stomach may indicate the presence of an energy vortex.

BIBLIOGRAPHY

Arkansas State Parks. Crater of Diamonds State Park. www.arkansasstateparks.com.

Arkansas. "Stoneflower Cottage." arkansas.com.

Bowden, Bill. "Glass Bottles Found behind 'Haunted' Arkansas Hotel Date to 1938 Cancer Elixir." *Arkansas Democrat-Gazette*, April 12, 2019. www.arkansasonline.com.

Crescent Hotel. "Crescent Hotel History." www.crescent-hotel.com.

Dean, Kimberly, and James Dean. *Pete the Cat's Groovy Guide to Life: Tips from a Cool Cat for Living an Awesome Life.* New York: HarperCollins, 2015.

DuBose, F., ed. *See the USA the Easy Way: 136 Loop Tours to 1200 Great Places.* Pleasantville, NY: Reader's Digest, 1995.

Elephant Sanctuary. www.elephantsanctuary.org.

Encyclopedia of Arkansas. encyclopediaofarkansas.net.

George, Don, ed. *By the Seat of My Pants: Humorous Tales of Travel and Misadventure.* Melbourne, AUS: Lonely Planet Global Ltd., 2016.

Haunted Places. hauntedplaces.org.

Lee, Brittney. "Getaway to the Boston Mountains." Only in Arkansas, May 6, 2018. onlyinark.com.

Missouri State Parks. "Grand Gulf State Park." mostateparks.com.

National Park Service. "Buffalo National River." www.nps.gov.

———. "Mesa Verde National Park, Colorado." www.nps.gov.

Native Languages of the Americas. (1998–2016). native-languages.org.

Scales, K. *House of a Hundred Rooms: Tales the Ghost Tour Guides Do Not Tell.* N.p.: self-published, 2017.

UFO Nut. www.ufonut.com.

University of Arkansas System. "Arkansas Archeological Survey." archeology. uark.edu.

War Eagle Mill. www.wareaglemill.com.

Wikipedia. "E. Fay Jones, Architect." en.wikipedia.org.

———. "Joplin Spooklight." en.wikipedia.org.

———. "Ozark Howler." en.wikipedia.org.

ABOUT THE AUTHOR

Cynthia McRoy Carroll, a self-confessed dreamer, enjoys visiting museums and traveling, obsessing over space between words and haunting the beaches of Galveston for glimpses of brown pelicans diving into cresting waves for fish.

Her maternal Ozark ancestors settled in Ozark country during the early 1800s and were among the first pioneers of Westward Expansion to privately own Ozark land. Other heritage traces to the legendary Dalton Gang, infamous train and bank robbers of the late 1800s. This unlikely ancestral mix of pioneers and outlaws gives rise to tendencies that range from passionate homesteading to the gypsy art of flying by the seat of one's pants.

With a passion for visual arts, she has been the tour and docent program coordinator for the Museum of Fine Arts Houston; a licensed interior designer; an art and design instructor for Lone Star College; and a docent for the Houston-area arts and design community. An honors graduate of Lone Stone College, she also attended the Glassell School of Art and currently participates in workshops and conferences exploring paranormal topics.

A gypsy-style childhood drives her interest in ghost tales and paranormal curiosities. Her childhood was spent in the historic St. Louis neighborhoods of Benton Park and Soulard, once boom-and-bust working-class slums that are now revitalized treasures listed on the National Trust for Historic Preservation.

She began writing later in life, first to work through an identity crisis after learning that her birth certificate father was not her biological father. Later, she wrote for enjoyment and soon won eight writing awards with the Writers of The Woodlands.